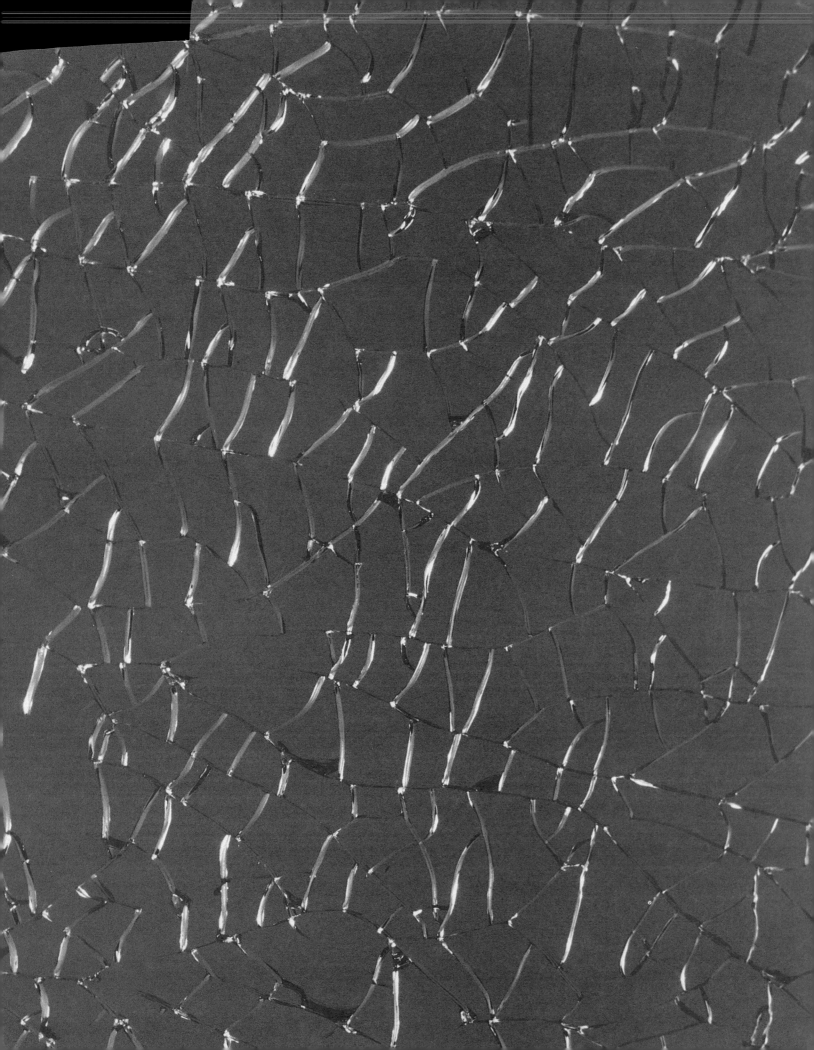

Shattering Notions

To Barbara —
Thank you for your dedication,
your creative ideas, and your time,
efforts and enthusiasm for glass
and glass history —
Anne Madarasz
July 30, 1998

GLASS
Shattering Notions

Anne Madarasz

A Companion to the Historical Society of Western
Pennsylvania Exhibition "Glass: Shattering Notions"
The Senator John Heinz Pittsburgh Regional History Center

Opening April 1998

Historical Society
of Western Pennsylvania

About this Book

Typeset in Cochin, Garamond, and Gill Sans.

Printing and Color Preparation by Hoechstetter Printing, Pittsburgh, Pennsylvania.

Smythe sewn binding by Pittsburgh Binding.

Design by Ron Donoughe.

Contents

Acknowledgements

By Anne Madarasz

This catalog, which was generously underwritten by the PPG Industries Foundation, and the exhibition it accompanies are the result of five years of inquiry into glass and the history of the glass industry in Western Pennsylvania. It is intended as the first general statement on the subject by the Historical Society since the institution's sponsorship of Lowell Innes' *Pittsburgh Glass 1797-1891* in the 1970s. It draws on a museum and archival collection originally developed under Innes' guidance that has been refined and expanded over the past five years.

Many people lent their expertise to the preparation of this catalog. From the beginning, I relied upon glass scholar Arlene Palmer Schwind, who shared rare source material, conducted research in the Dun Records, located objects and archival materials, and commented on the manuscript. I am also indebted to industrial historian Philip Scranton, who read the manuscript and contributed the introduction. Ellen Denker commented at length on the text; her insights on design were particularly helpful. Dean Six reviewed the text and shared his understandings of the development of the regional industry. Throughout the project, Richard O'Connor, Gay Taylor at Wheaton Village, and Holly McCluskey at Oglebay Institute have shared their research, opened their archives, and answered a thousand questions. Thanks also to Mary Miller at the Carnegie Library, who shared her patent research, Audrey Iacone who discovered and shared

important documents, the librarians at the Corning Museum who tirelessly chased quotes and sources not available locally, and the entire staff at the Annex of the Carnegie Library who opened their stacks to us.

Special thanks should go to Frank A. Archinaco, Executive Vice President of PPG Industries, Inc., Roslyn Rosenblatt at the PPG Industries Foundation, and the Board of Directors of PPG Industries Foundation for believing in this project. Other individuals instrumental in this publication include Katherine Grier for her thoughts on glass and culture; Regina Blacszyck, who shared her unpublished dissertation; Jane Shadel Spillman at the Corning Museum; Ken Wilson; The Hunt Library of Carnegie Mellon University; employees at PPG Industries — Pat Corsi, David Green, Chuck Greenburg, Linn Noah, Sue Patterson, Troy Jayroe, and Karen Welsh; James and Bruce Stephens at Kopp Glass, Inc.; American Video Glass Co.; Sony, especially Michael Koff and Erin Walsh; Paul and Irene Sailer; Kirk Weaver; Glenshaw Glass Co., especially James Martin, Henrietta Garrett, Tom and Isabelle Pears, Marion Palmer; the Hillman Library at the University of Pittsburgh; Robert Batto; members of local glass clubs too numerous to mention; and the members of the Glass Exhibit Advisory Committee, JoAnne and Earl Autenreith, Allan Bierman, Jeff Conover, Mary Ferson, Gay Gabriel, Margaret Harmon, Olga Melograne, Bobbi Michaels, Charles Moore, Elizabeth Prine, Edith Putanko, Mary Quasey, Dean Six, and Frances Taylor.

The publication would not have been the same without the guidance and care given by Editor Paul Roberts, and his and designer Ron Donoughe's creative efforts and long hours. The photography is the work of Matt Bulvony and Brian Chisholm; their time and efforts are obvious. Jennifer Smith managed the photography; her excellent eye and schooled sense of design and color made everything shine. Margot Critchfield ably handled the indexing chores.

Museum Director Bill Keyes oversaw the exhibition project. Conservators Bruce Christman and Christine Daulton prepared the collection and Registrar Kathleen Wendell and her assistants, Linda Pelan and Bill Kindelan, made sure the collection was available and looking its best at all times. As well as contributing the preface, Chief Curator Ellen Rosenthal has been a guiding light in this project; under her leadership the exhibit and the catalog came to fruition. Historian Liz Watkins read the many drafts of the catalog and offered insightful comments that helped shape my thinking at key points. Interns Ed Slavishak, Kathy Mulvaney, and Liz Nohra shared in the research for both the book and the exhibit. Staff in the Historical Society's Library and Archives were important resources: Steve Doell, Rene Savits, and Art Louderback managed the archival photography. Library Division Director Carolyn Schumacher with Steve Doell also wrote company biographies and Sharon Watson-Mauro, Craig Moore, and Art Louderback fact-checked them. Lauren Uhl managed the production and writing of the company biographies. Other writers included Ellen Rosenthal and myself. Tracy Walther ably managed fabrication of the exhibit and the design team at Christopher Chadbourne & Associates, especially Chris and Tony Treu, and the fabrication team from EXPLUS, Inc., brought our ideas to life.

The catalog and the exhibit would not have succeeded without the dedicated fundraising efforts of Betty Arenth and Audrey Brourman. The primary benefactor for the exhibition was The Hillman Foundation, Inc. Foundation President Ron Wertz offered support and, at pivotal times, new ways to consider interpretation and display. Other contributors to the exhibit, at the Patron level, include: Eden Hall Foundation; The Mary Hillman Jennings Foundation; KDKA - TV 2; PPG Industries Foundation; and Sony Technology Center-Pittsburgh. Contributors:

American Video Glass Company; Paul & Dina Block Foundation/Pittsburgh Post-Gazette; Eichleay Foundation; The Glencairn Foundation; The Roy A. Hunt Foundation; The Thomas Phillips Johnson & Jane Moore Johnson Foundation; Mrs. Thomas J. Lewis, Jr.; and the Pennsylvania Historical and Museum Commission. Donors: AGR International, Inc.; Baltimore Glass Club; Mr. & Mrs. Robert Barensfeld; Bozzone Family Foundation; The Ciloets; Corning Inc. Foundation; Dr. Clifton Dietz; E.I. DuPont de Nemours; Ellwood City Area Historical Society; Mr. & Mrs. James A. Fisher; Mr. & Mrs. James Frank; FMC Corporation Chemical Products Group; Mrs. William D. Gordon; H.C. Fry Glass Club; Historical Glass Club of Pittsburgh; Michael D. LaBate II; National American Glass Club Pittsburgh Chapter; Pennsylvania Society of Land Surveyors-Southwest Chapter; Rainbow Diamond Depression Glass Club; The Donald & Sylvia Robinson Family Foundation; Rosedale Community Club; Dean Six; Solutia Inc.; Tg Soda Ash, Inc.; Florence Irene Thomas; Bertha E. Thompson Memorial Gifts; Three Rivers Depression Era Glass Society; TRACO; Tri-State Depression Era Glass Society; Twentieth Century Questers; Unimin Corporation; and United Jewish Federation Foundation.

I have had two constant partners through the life of this project. My partner at work, Lauren Uhl, researched factory histories, catalogued thousands of objects, tracked down images, worked the Internet to locate images and objects, and did a thousand other tasks small and large. My partner at home, Tom Miller, read the manuscript countless times, attended more glass shows than he cares to remember, gave up evenings and weekends, and was never anything but supportive. This book is dedicated to them.

Anne Madarasz is Curator at the Historical Society of Western Pennsylvania, and was Project Director and Curator for the glass exhibition.

Preface

By Ellen Rosenthal

Historians consider glassmaking America's earliest industry. In 1608, just one year after the colonists arrived from England, they established a glass factory in Jamestown, Virginia. Although the Jamestown works failed, the industry took hold in New Jersey, Maryland, and New York in the mid-1700s. New England manufactories followed. Western Pennsylvania, with two glassworks operating by 1797, was not far behind.

The glass industry shared responsibility for establishing Pittsburgh's reputation in the early 1800s as "the dirtiest town in the United States." A French traveler, Michel Chevalier, described the city as "surrounded... with a dense black smoke which bursting forth in volumes from the foundries, forges, glasshouses... falls in flakes of soot upon the dwellings... of the inhabitants."[1] For nearly a century, the Pittsburgh region was the production and marketing heart of America's glass industry. Today, Pittsburgh is better known for steel and iron, but the city's glass legacy is equally rich. Just as Pittsburgh made the steel for America's bridges, Pittsburgh produced the glass for globes that lit the nation's streets, for the windows of the country's homes and store fronts, and for the jars that held the foodstuffs to feed a growing urban population.

This book is the companion catalogue to "Glass: Shattering Notions," an exhibit at the Senator John Heinz Pittsburgh Regional History Center which opened on April 25, 1998, and was the first major exhibit to present glass as the product of industry. Earlier exhibitions of glass, mounted primarily in art museums, included only glass tableware and novelties, and focused on design and attribution. The Historical Society's exhibit and catalogue present the full scope of the region's industrial output, from beautiful cut glass tableware to utilitarian products such as window panes and fruit jars. Given equal consideration is the value of glass as a consumer product, influenced by such factors as market demand and preference, technological advances, and trade competition. Both exhibit and catalogue track the vagaries of the glass business, documenting labor practices, marketing challenges and opportunities, and factory failures and successes.

The "Shattering Notions" title refers to two misconceptions: that the Steel City produced only steel, and that aesthetics is the sole criterion for inclusion of glass in museums. Glass displayed in the exhibit and the book provides a "window" for visitors onto the intricate interplay between industrial production, economic conditions, historical events, and social trends. The exhibit spotlights the luminous beauty of glass, while stressing its origin. Visitors and readers can see that even the most exquisite, delicately pressed glass emerged from a gritty factory.

"Shattering Notions" reflects the Historical Society's commitment to scholarly research and to the presentation of artifacts in historical context, but neither the exhibit nor the catalogue attempts to be encyclopedic. The industry has lasted for over 200 years, surviving many changes. Our goal is to offer insight into glass and the glass industry for both a general audience and for knowledgeable collectors.

The idea for this exhibit originated with former Executive Director John Herbst (1986-1997), who recognized the importance of the Historical Society's extensive collection of regional glass.

That collection itself was the result of Charles A. McClintock's efforts to expand glass holding when he was Historical Society President in the 1940s and '50s. In 1951, McClintock appealed to all Society members to donate local glass: "It is the plan of The Historical Society to expand its present modest display of Pittsburgh glass into a comprehensive and permanent collection."[2] Lowell Innes, the renowned, pioneering glass historian and author of *Pittsburgh Glass, 1797-1891: A History and Guide for Collectors* (Houghton Mifflin, 1976), aided in McClintock's effort by enlisting the support of glass collectors. He also generated public interest in Western Pennsylvania glass when in the 1940s he mounted three exhibitions at the Carnegie Museum of Art in Pittsburgh. By the time of John Herbst's tenure, the collection had grown to nearly 3,000 objects. An additional 1,200 objects have been added to the collection since the glass exhibit project began.

The glass collection remained largely uncatalogued, that is unrecorded, until 1992, when work on this exhibit began. The first task of Project Curator Anne Madarasz was to review, photograph, and attribute all 3,000 pieces of glass. Her second project was to uncover the full scope of the industry. This involved researching glass factories and their owners, as well as workers and merchants in city directories, insurance maps, town chronicles, personal and business papers, and published sources. Her nearly photographic memory and superb research skills allowed her to identify gaps in both the object and archival collections. She targeted and acquired glass, primarily through donation, building a fine collection into a great collection. Glass documentation grew proportionately, as Madarasz brought in the archives of companies, design drawings such as those from the Rudy Brothers Stained Glass Studio, product catalogues, and the papers of glasshouse owners and workers. Research of this type requires immersion in the details. Even so, Madarasz surfaced at the end still committed to distilling facts into a clear and engaging storyline. She has made an important contribution to our understanding of the industrial history of the region.

Other scholars of glass, industrial development, and material culture generously provided their expertise. Arlene Palmer Schwind, one of the nation's leading glass scholars, consulted early in the project, advising on glass attributions, cataloguing, and research. She contributed information on the development of the region's industry from her research on 17th and 18th century factories and glass marketing. Ken Wilson, former curator of glass at the Henry Ford Museum, had organized the Historical Society's glass and installed a display at our former headquarters in 1986. He generously shared his research on the collection.

Six scholars guided exhibit development. Philip Scranton, Ph.D., Georgia Tech, brought to bear his extensive knowledge of the country's industries and his personal experience with this region's glass mills. Katherine Grier, Ph.D., University of Utah, saw the project through the eyes of a material culture analyst and exhibit developer. She encouraged the exhibit team to look at the broader cultural significance of glass. Richard O'Connor, Ph.D., U.S. Department of the Interior, who wrote his doctoral dissertation on the technology of glassmaking, reviewed our explanations of technological change and its implications. With expertise on Western Pennsylvania history and geography, Edward K. Muller, Ph.D., University of Pittsburgh, offered advice on the use of maps and the presentation of the glassmaking system. Regina Blacszyck, Ph.D., Boston University, author of a forthcoming book on the marketing of glass and ceramics, made valuable suggestions about the expansion of glass markets, and the sphere of the Pittsburgh region's glass factories. Ellen Paul Denker used her knowledge of the American ceramics industry, which parallels the glass industry, to comment on the exhibit and the catalogue.

Two museum educators and an audience research evaluator also reviewed plans for the exhibit. Beth Twiss-Garrity, an educator at the H.F. duPont Winterthur Museum, shared her skills in the interpretation of material culture. Cynthia Clegg, Museum of Early Trades and Crafts, has experience explaining manufacturing processes and trade to visitors of all ages. Randi Korn, Randi Korn and Associates, considered the visitor's perspective in her exhibit critique. Pamela Fahlund, a marketing professional with 20 years of experience with profit and nonprofit organizations, suggested ideas for interesting the public in glassmaking and glass history.

The designers at Christopher Chadbourne and Associates, Cambridge, Massachusetts, especially Tony Treu, Chris Chadbourne, and Bill Ruggeri, gave energy and form to our concepts. With evocative displays, and challenging but fun interactive components, the exhibit pleases every visitor from the active first-grader to the glass specialist.

The Historical Society's Board of Trustees supported this project over its five-year course. William C. King, Vice-Chairman of the Board, and Hax McCullough, trustee and noted historian, carefully read the manuscript and made numerous recommendations. Former trustee David C. Green, Director of Corporate Communications for PPG Industries, Inc., checked the manuscript for accuracy regarding the history of the corporation. He also compiled up-to-date information on the current state of the company for the exhibit and the catalogue.

Undertakings as substantial as these could only be accomplished with the assistance of many other Historical Society staff members. Special Project Associate Lauren Uhl catalogued glass, scoured city directories, and searched deeds and newspapers for information about manufacturers. She also organized the exhibit matrix of over 1,000 objects and images. Exhibit Associate Jennifer Smith, with an unerring sense of color and form, supervised photography for the catalogue, managed graphics for the exhibit, and assisted in many other ways. Museum Director William Keyes supervised and participated in conceptual and design development. Historian Elizabeth Watkins, Ph.D., read and commented on the manuscript, edited labels, participated in design development and assisted with interactive elements of the exhibit. Special Project Associate Tracy Walther coordinated the fabrication and installation of the exhibit. Registrar Kathleen Wendell and the assistants under her supervision, Linda Pelan and Bill Kindelan, managed the countless details of new acquisitions, loans, conservation, and object installation. Fundraising Consultant Audrey Brourman and Betty Arenth, Acting Director of the Historical Society, worked energetically to secure funding for the project. Ann Fortescue, Director of Education, brought the educator's perspective to the exhibit development team. Interns from the Cooperstown Museum Studies Program, Elizabeth Nohra, Hillary Krueger, and Kathy Mulvaney, developed education programs, pursued research, and acted as administrative assistants. Other staff members who contributed to the project include: Trish Beatty, Public Relations Coordinator; Barbara Budde, School & Family Programs Coordinator; Lynne Conner,

Director of Stages in History; Robert Digby, Volunteer Coordinator; Steve Doell, Head of Processing; Marilyn Erwin, Director of Publications; Ann Fortescue, Director of Education; Cathy Fratto, former Italian-American Program Coordinator; Bill Kindelan, Museum Assistant; Gail Lovelady, Advancement Associate; Paula Mahoney, Museum Shop Manager; Doug McCombs, Assistant Curator; Gary Pollock, former Assistant Curator; Rob DeOrio, Development Department Manager; Chrisoula Randaz Perdziola, Adult Programs; Sylvia Turner, Director of Marketing; Carolyn Schumacher, Director, Library and Archives. The following interns helped in many different ways: Jackie Kaiser, Rachel Mihalovich, Sheila Pozon, Kim Root, Christina M. Simms, Edward Slavishak, Bonnie Weimer.

The catalogue was ably shepherded from conception to publication by Historical Society Editor Paul Roberts, who also edited and polished the exhibit labels. The catalogue's designer was Ron Donoughe of Pittsburgh.

Major grants from The Hillman Foundation, Inc., for research, planning, acquisition and implementation made this ambitious exhibition possible. Ronald W. Wertz, President of the foundation, expertly monitored the exhibit's development, using his first hand experience with the Hillman Hall of Gems at the Carnegie Museum of Natural History, Pittsburgh. The exhibit has greatly benefited from his watchfulness and perceptive suggestions. This catalogue was underwritten by a grant from PPG Industries Foundation. Roslyn Rosenblatt, the Foundation's Executive Director, immediately recognized the importance of documenting the glassmaking heritage of Western Pennsylvania. I trust the reader will as well.

Ellen Rosenthal is Chief Curator at the Historical Society of Western Pennsylvania.

[1] Michel Chevalier, *Society, Manners and Politics in the United States: Being a Series of Letters on North America* (Weeks, Jordan and Co., 1839), 128-71, *passim.*
[2] "Historical Society Notes," in *The Western Pennsylvania Historical Magazine*, 1951: 4, 279.

Introduction

By Philip Scranton

While reading Anne Madarasz's vigorous and inviting review of Western Pennsylvania glassmaking across two centuries, I was drawn back to the summer of 1966 and my brief and only visit to the Rochester Glass works, just across the lazy Beaver River from my parents' home in Beaver County. It was August, a month before I would return to college and occupy my first apartment. Despite summer earnings and a cheaper-than-dormitory rent ($60/month), I had hardly any money to spend on furnishing the apartment's two tiny rooms. Hence, I urged my aged Chrysler New Yorker up a narrow lane to Rochester Glass' factory salesroom, the back of which was crammed with discontinued styles and dusty seconds. I needed cheap glassware and, for about $3, gathered a boxful of mismatched tumblers, mugs, and stemware — "just the ticket," as my dad would say. My mother was silent, doubtless horrified at the "taste" my selections revealed.

Shattering Notions has led me to reflect on that tiny experience, and on the relative invisibility of the glass industry in the Pittsburgh region — and I grew up in the midst of the industry. In those decades, it seemed that everyone's job in my hometown revolved around the steel corporations and other metal works in the valley (St. Joe Lead, Hussey Copper), refining and fabricating metal, hauling materials in and goods out, managing the flows, and selling to and buying for or from such companies. Giant companies and huge plants (like J&L's 8-mile monster along the Ohio River at Aliquippa), and big unions and bitter strikes (like 1959's memorable 116-day walkout) dominated the landscape of experience. School groups toured steel mills (we went to Crucible Steel in Midland), while parents worked in and around them (my

dad at USS in engineering). Yet, tucked into every corner of the "Pittsburgh District," scores of area glassworks had created an industrial concentration just as significant to their trade nationally as were the region's metal-producing facilities. Few of us noticed the glassmakers then, and relatively few historians have paid much attention in the last generation. This exhibition and this catalogue will go a long way toward ending a durable silence about a fascinating, significant, and complex industry.

Let us take a few mintues to consider this industry in some detail. Glass artifacts have had a compelling appeal for centuries, even millennia. In a sense, the millions of collectors who gather and preserve fine and ordinary glass (from Tiffany and Pairpoint to insulators and souvenirs) are the democratized successors to Roman, Byzantine, and Venetian grandees and their wondrous assemblages of ancient, medieval, and early modern glass. Yet beyond this aesthetic appreciation, glass holds two other dimensions of fascination — as a substance and as a manufacturing process.

Materially, glass is a majestically curious product of long-mysterious arts. As explained in a handbook by Pittsburgh Plate Glass' C. J. Phillips (*Glass: The Miracle Maker*, 1948), this magical stuff has very peculiar properties. When its components are heated together properly, they fuse into a viscous (thick liquid) mass that proves manipulable over a large temperature range and that, on cooling, hardens into a rigid shape without crystallizing or decomposing into its constituents. (Milk, for instance, does not do this; if unhomogenized milk is frozen, the butterfat separates from the skim and it's a devil of a job to mix them up again, as I remember from Pittsburgh winters in the 1950s). Glass stabilizes at whatever form it settles into; the fusion takes and holds. Its components have blended into something new, which after being shaped in its viscous state, becomes permanent and often both beautiful and functional. Glass' resistance to heat, cold, weather, and most chemical agents is fair compensation for its vulnerability to physical shocks (brittleness), a weakness that technical innovators have remedied when necessary (i.e., auto safety glass, or tempered glass for architectural and furnishing uses). Glass bonds nicely with metal, which makes both light bulbs and scientific instruments feasible. Yet it has no basic chemical composition and can be made into virtually endless varieties. Though something similar can be said of materials like pottery, brick, and tile, the transparency of glass and its affective links with cultural sensibilities mark it as particularly special. (I'd warrant, without fear of contradiction, that the numbers of American brick collectors are far fewer than those seeking glass.) As a material, its fascination complements the vibrations resonating from artifacts.

Glassmaking is a remarkable process. Most glass has long been composed of three humble materials: silica (usually sand), soda (sodium oxide), and lime (calcium oxide), commonly in proportions by weight, respectively, of 100, 40, and 25. Heated together, these materials fuse at a temperature appreciably lower than would be necessary to melt silica without its partners (about 1340°F), a level readily reached by ancient fires, first perhaps 9,000 years ago. Indeed, to make modern, nearly pure-silica glass (the "high crystal form"), a robustly built furnace must reach 3100°F. Molten glass accommodates those who would work it. It accumulates in gummy, but mobile masses, which glassworkers can gather into balls for blowing, or draw into rods, sheets and tubes, or pour into receptacles (molds) where, with pressure, it fills every cranny. (A 17th century commentator observed: "'tis tenacious and sticks together.") Like textiles, it takes color eagerly, turning green when iron oxides enter the melting batch or a rich blue when cobalt is added (1 part cobalt to 100,000 parts of the batch will do the trick: think of a teaspoon and a good-sized hot tub). Moreover, skilled workers can swirl together or layer molten glasses of different colors without their hues mixing. To an observer, glassmaking can present a primal ballet of creation (fire, heat, and danger, the blower's pipe and delicate touch) or a sorcerer's apprentice parade of endlessly duplicated bottles for beer and pop. Either way, it's mesmerizing.

As artifact, material, and process, glass exercises its fascination, while as a business, Pittsburgh-area and national glass production was and remains significant to America's industrialization. This review also comes in three parts, concerning industrial districts, economics, and innovation. As the catalogue documents, the Tri-State long represented American glassmaking's most spatially concentrated production complex. Such clusters are known as industrial districts, regional groupings of companies from tiny to huge that were often initially triggered by concentrations of essential materials, labor and capital, or marketing potentials. Philadelphia's prominence in both specialty textiles and metalworking, for example, depended heavily on the city being a destination for immigrant skilled workers and on its effective railway connections north, south, and west. In Michigan, Grand Rapids' fine furniture industry arose first as a means to convert local hardwoods into products with far higher value than raw lumber. The origins of Pittsburgh glass mix the Michigan case with the Quaker City's experience, for it was good sand and cheap fuel, abetted by easy river transport to the west, that drew the first generation of entrepreneurs to the three rivers' confluence. Workers soon followed (some of whom aspired to and reached plant ownership) and a developmental synergy arose, then burst into full flower in the later 19th century when vast, local natural gas resources came "onstream." Shop-experienced "factory graduates" then headed most of the region's glassworks, succeeding able but more technically limited pioneers.

Although these proprietors competed vigorously and supported a variety of small business "auxiliaries" (e.g., machinery and mold-makers, and contract designers), they also formed institutions for the common good of the trade — most notably, coalitions that sponsored the annual Pittsburgh glass expositions to organize the market, beginning in the 1880s. These collective selling venues were crucial to the profitability of specialty and styled goods makers, for they saved makers' marketing costs and gave buyers the chance to view hundreds of novelties in a few days. (A comparable furniture exposition commenced at Grand Rapids in the same decade.) Organizing the market gave additional impetus to industrial concentration in the region. Much of the nation's household goods production emerged from similar clusters: fashion textiles from Philadelphia; finished clothing from New York; jewelry from New York and Providence; and furniture from Chicago, Grand Rapids, and several eastern cities. In this context, Pittsburgh's regional glass manufacture stands as another fully realized example of locally based resources building a powerful and productive industrial district.

In the national economy, glassmaking never achieved the centrality that agriculture or steel maintained, but this was no minor sector. For example, as the Great Depression ended in 1939, glass ranked just outside the top 10 percent of American manufacturing groups — 38th among the 351 that the U.S. Census Bureau surveyed, with total output of $320 million. At the turn of the 20th century, glass firms employed about 60,000 workers, a figure that rose to over 80,000 by the early 1920s, then drooped to 69,000 in 1925. The Depression, of course, temporarily shrank factory complements, but in 1939, 70,000 Americans devoted their energies to making glass at the 229 firms which survived the long slump. That force more than doubled by the late 1940s to 150,000, spurred first by war and then by revived consumer demand. Their output in all segments of the trade reached $590 million in 1946.

Between 1900 and the mid-1920s, glass production had doubled in volume, thanks chiefly to technological changes. (The workforce grew 39 percent, while active horsepower, a good indication of technical intensification, jumped 350 percent). During the 1920s construction boom, the glass used in windows amounted to over 500 million square-feet yearly — that's a lot of houses and buildings — and plate glass output reached 94 million square-feet annually, while over 20 million gross of bottles and jars, or 288 million units, sped from U.S. factories. Pressed and blown glass manufacturing soared as well, to 70 million dozen pieces in 1923, and advanced even to higher plateaus later in the decade.

By the mid-1950s, the number of active enterprises reached past 400, though, again due to technical advances, the glass workforce had contracted over 20 percent, to 115,000. Value added in manufacturing (the source of profits), stood at $182 million in 1925, but reached $926 million in 1954 and $1.1 billion in 1958. Two years later, the glass companies included in the *Fortune* 500 posted the highest annual return on investment among the 15 industry groups evaluated (13.2 percent). The value of pressed and blown glass alone in 1960 represented four-fifths of the whole industry's total for 1946, and the production of bottles and jars reached a staggering 160 million gross (11.4 billion units). Headed by Pittsburgh Plate Glass, Corning, and Libbey-Owens-Ford, the glass industry was a significant player in America's post-war economic success. Meanwhile, hundreds of smaller enterprises generated bulk goods, stylish novelties, and custom-made glass products. Glass was many little businesses comprising a large industry.

Innovation is a less-quantifiable element of significance. Plainly, as you will see, patents bubbled forth from the Pittsburgh area in the 19th century, and local firms quickly adopted novel techniques invented elsewhere (like the Siemens continuous melting tank). Meanwhile, Pittsburgh's glass exposition surely represented a broadly important advance on the marketing side. Equally valuable, a regional firm started one of the first glass research and development units, late in the 1800s, and yielded new procedures for making window glass that were the product of a decade's dedication by John Lubber. Pittsburgh Plate Glass extended the research informing innovation in the new century, devising reliable means to cast and temper sheets of glass, and a good deal more. Yet the fact that the mainstream of technical creativity diverged from the Pittsburgh district about 1900 must be noted. Midwestern glassmakers fashioned the machinery for continuous "mechanical" processing of bottles, and New York's Corning commenced its trajectory of technical novelties by 1904 with the first version of Pyrex. Pittsburgh Plate Glass' Phillips, while crediting his own firm with key innovations, could not avoid awarding laurels to Corning for a series of exceptional advances that moved glassmaking's technological capabilities to new levels (precision tube-making, automatic light bulb blowing, 96 percent silica glass). The leading corporations' innovative momentum continues to the present (Corning's fiber optics division alone generating billions in sales), fueled by extensive R&D efforts and joint ventures that keep them globally competitive and technologically significant.

The glass trade is complex both practically and historically. Its processes demanded huge quantities of inexpensive but heavy raw materials (a supply and transportation issue) that were also relatively free from impurities that would alter the product in undesirable ways (a technical challenge). Glassmaking was and is energy-intensive, hence the search for locations with cheap fuel at hand; yet it is also unforgiving, for "fixing" errors in production or fabrication are impossible. Finished goods faced fresh hazards once they entered distribution channels; unless packed and handled carefully, they could arrive at their destinations as boxes and barrels of fragments. Little wonder that glassmakers closely followed innovations in shock-absorbent packaging (from early corrugated paper cartons to the Styrofoam "popcorns" and plastic bubble wraps of the present-day).

For generations, glassmaking demanded a daily blending, not only of materials, but also of highly skilled and barely skilled workers, of veteran artisans and novice boys. Experienced workers long-sustained vigorous unions, exercised shopfloor control of output, and managed the careful transmission of craft knowledge. In this context, technical innovation generated factory conflicts, as when owners sought to meet exploding demand by introducing machines to speed production of standard goods (bottles, tumblers). In consequence, from the 1880s through the Great Depression, the industry experienced complex struggles concerning technological change, workplace authority, and job security.

Furthermore, the glass trades' complexity is compounded by the extraordinary diversity of its products and markets. Until the late 19th century, demand derived from traditional sources: residential and commercial construction (for windows and plate); other industries (bottles and containers, railway signal glass); and ornamental, household, and business activity (stained glass, tableware, lampshades, and chimneys). Some markets called for huge volumes of staple goods (windows, beer bottles), while others required smaller quantities for high quality products (signal glass, mirrors, lamp globes) or stylish novelties ("upmarket" table glass and giftware). This, in turn, shaped some firms and trade divisions dedicated to achieving versions of mass production, while encouraging others to emphasize style and quality over price considerations, each approach having its own technical and marketing implications.

With the Second Industrial Revolution, this portrait became even more complex. The burgeoning chemical industry needed highly specialized glass for its plants and laboratories, whereas the electrical trades demanded millions of bulbs and insulators. Electrified advertising brought a boom in neon specialties, and radio propelled the fabrication of mass-produced vacuum tubes. Cameras and, in time, motion pictures, called for precision optical glasses and the automotive trades soon became major customers, with the toll of accidents leading toward roadside reflectors, automatic stoplights and PPG's "sandwich" (laminated) safety glass. Modern architecture relied on innovations in glass panels and blocks (glass was even used for floors, though not widely). Affluence built markets for designer glass (Steuben), while increased vacation travel generated demand for souvenir glass in thousands of varieties. Scientific research added to the specialty end of the industry, most notably before World War II, with the 200-inch lens for the Mount Palomar astronomical observatory, but in countless other ways as well.

This explosion of uses continued in the postwar decades, but new complications arose as well. The pace of invention hardly slackened (picture tubes for TVs and, later, computer screens and fiber optics), yet several of glass' traditional markets stagnated or shrank (think of beer *cans* and *plastic* pop bottles). By the 1960s, when I dropped in at Rochester Glass, the great era of Pittsburgh's regional glass production was rapidly fading, even as its hallmark firm (PPG) had become a global anchor. That complex transition is perhaps the final element in the tale which this exhibit and catalogue brings to light.

Illuminating two centuries of glass history and the Tri-State region's centrality to the industry's development represents an important contribution to deepening public understanding of the profound connections between technology, design, work, business, and a very special place. We all owe a debt of gratitude to the exhibition's and to this catalogue's underwriters and to the Historical Society's staff, whose support and professionalism have made reconstructing this world of glass possible. I hope you find your encounter with it fascinating, and along the way, savor the significance and complexity of its history.

Philip Scranton is Kranzberg Professor of the History of Technology at Georgia Tech.

Glass made in the Pittsburgh region is all

around us. The next time you're stopped at a

traffic light, or take a train, or land at any

airport in the world, look for Pittsburgh glass.

Now, to learn how it all began, go to the

next page!

Signals and lenses by Kopp Glass, Swissvale, Pa. (1965-1995)

CHAPTER 1

SHATTERING
NOTIONS

Overview

*Opposite page: Great heat
and everyday ingredients —
sand, ash, and lime — create
the miracle material glass,
shown flowing molten red
from a furnace at a U.S. Glass
Co. factory in Glassport, Pa., c.
1950. No matter whether the
object is hand-formed (right,
goblet, c. 1925) or mass-
produced, all glass starts with
the super-heating of simple
elements. Inset, opposite page:
Work crew at McKee Glass, c.
1920, Jeannette, Pa.*

While the story of glass in America began at
Jamestown in 1608, almost 200 years passed before
skilled glassworkers crossed the Allegheny Mountains
to begin production in Western Pennsylvania. Since
1797, when the region's first two glasshouses were
founded, the conical furnace stacks of glass factories
have been a defining feature of the region's
skyline. Scores of glasshouses followed, producing rivers of glass for an abundant variety
of uses sold throughout the nation and, in
time, around the world. By the Civil War,
Western Pennsylvania was the center of the
nation's glass industry.

A generation later, Pittsburgh glass was everywhere: as tile for the walls of New York's great transportation tunnels; in searchlights on the Panama
Canal; as insulators for endless miles of telephone
and telegraph wire; in "Liberty lens"

headlights of Ford automobiles; yet, in addition to the countless industrial applications for Pittsburgh's products, glassmakers in the city were also commissioned to make fine tableware for five presidents in the 19th century. From the magnificent to the mundane, from intricately engraved tumblers designed as singular presentation pieces, to bottles by the boxcar, Pittsburgh made it. The city's gas and electric streetlights, lamps, and lamp chimneys lit the world. Its railway and traffic signals brought order to an industrializing nation's frenzy. Its plate glass provided windows for many countries and helped make possible the department store and the shop fronts of our consumer economy. Store fronts of Carrara glass, basement windows of glass block, plate glass windows for the great palaces of consumption — the uses for glass were endless.

The very creation of glass seems miraculous. As Samuel Johnson remarked in 1752, "Who[,] when he first saw the sand or ashes... melted into a metallic form... would have imagined that, in this shapeless lump, lay concealed so many conveniences of life?"[1] The miracle occurs when tiny grains of sand are melted at heat approaching 2,500°F, forming the molten mass from which glass is shaped. The process can occur in nature — when lightning strikes a beach, or in a volcanic eruption — but it is man who harnessed the formula for art and industry. In an intricate ballet performed for thousands of years, using the hot breath of life and simple metal tools, man has teased from the fiery mass a multitude of forms. While the interplay of fire and form has occurred in Western Pennsylvania for just 200 years, the region's impact on glass history has, nonetheless, been enormous.

Top: The earliest products were utilitarian wares, such as this jug jar, and glass, all traced to glass-works in the Fayette County area, 1800 to 1845; iron in the sand caused the green tint of the finished glass. Bottom: This image, found hidden behind a framed photo in a South Side home, shows a crew of men and boys working with simple metal tools and a hand press, c. 1910.

Pittsburgh's strategic location on the inland river system, with the Allegheny Mountains to the east and the nation's future to the west, positioned the city ideally for the manufacture of this fragile product. Both of the earliest glass factories in the region — the New Geneva Glass Works of Albert Gallatin, 45 miles southeast of Pittsburgh in Fayette County, and the Pittsburgh Glass Works of James O'Hara and Isaac Craig — relied on the river network for trade. While Pittsburgh glasshouses experimented with marketing products in the East and, as early as the 1820s, even shipped goods to Central and South America, it was the Louisiana Purchase of 1803 that dramatically stimulated markets in the western half of North America. (The 1803 land deal with France brought an additional 885,000 square miles under American control.)

Between 1800 and 1850, the population in the western U.S. grew from 300,000 to over 5 million, while the population nationally exploded from 5.3 million to 23.3 million. As Pittsburgh assumed its position as outfitter to settlers bound for the nation's interior, the rugged Allegheny Mountains to the east also provided some protection from cheaper European imports and the eastern glasshouses. Growth in the industry, however, was by no means constant, and business partnerships in the region formed and dissolved continually in the early years.

Exploding demand for glass coincided with the introduction of press mold technology to the factory floor in the late 1820s, revolutionizing the industry. Using these hand presses, glass could be made more quickly and the forms could be standardized. This American innovation found wide application in Pittsburgh factories, and the city would eventually become the pressed glass capital of the nation. By 1837, 28 factories called the region home, with 15 sited in and around Pittsburgh, and another 13 found along the rivers in the outlying counties of Fayette and Washington.

Glass production expanded again during the Civil War years after William Leighton, Sr., of Wheeling, in present-day West Virginia, substituted cheap,

Designs on glass objects could be standardized using molds and presses. Many early patterns, such as "Loop" popularized by J.B. Lyon & Co. (1860-1895), mimicked the geometric decorative quality of cut glass. The lamp chimney's rounded flute magnified light.

plentiful soda lime for more expensive lead in the formula for colorless glass. When coupled with the technological innovation of pressing, his chemical innovation ensured that decorated or patterned glassware could be made inexpensively, opening the market for a new class of consumers. The quality of some of this pressed ware was fine enough that a British craftsman remarked,

> J.B. Lyon and Co., Pittsburgh, U.S. exhibit articles in moulded glass superior to any I have ever seen. It is impossible to detect the marks of the mould. The wine-glasses are as thin at top as if made by hand, showing that it is possible, by careful manipulation in pressing to make moulded glass equally fine as by handwork.[2]

By 1865, there were 45 glasshouses in Pittsburgh, many utilizing these new technologies. They produced a wide range of glass that could be shipped to markets far and wide using the rail system. Only 15 years later, in 1880, Allegheny County — specifically, Pittsburgh — had no rival. The stacks of 51 factories loomed over the landscape. One-quarter of the nation's glass factories, producing almost 30 per cent of America's glass, was found in the county, with 10 other factories in the region surrounding it. The volume of glass pouring from these factories was astounding. The Rochester Tumbler Co., northwest of Pittsburgh in Beaver County, boasted in 1886 that it was the "largest pressed glassworks in the world."[3] The firm turned out 45,000 *dozen* tumblers a week — 540,000 drinking glasses from just one factory in one week. Contemporary accounts of the region's bottle works, flat glasshouses, and glass novelty producers read much the same:

> There has just gone into operation at the corner on 27th and Smallman streets, this city, a glass factory for the manufacture of glass balls for trap shooting. Messrs. Brown & Agnew are the proprietors.... Working three shops at present, the output of the factory is 8,000 to 10,000 balls per day of as fine amber glass as is made in the country. The working forces will be increased next week, and the product will be raised to 16,000 balls per day.[4]

The discovery of natural gas and the spreading tentacles of rail lines fueled the region's growth even more in the late 19th century. Factories sprung up where once there was farmland, as new glass towns with names like Ford City and Jeannette were born. The larger Ohio Valley region — Western Pennsylvania, West Virginia, Ohio, and even Illinois and Indiana —

courted glass factory owners with offers of free gas and open land. To advertise plentiful gas, the town of Findlay, Ohio, went so far as to hang a banner proclaiming, "Findlay women chop no wood." Furnaces were fired throughout the Midwest, and by 1920, glass output in West Virginia and Ohio, when combined with Western Pennsylvania's, accounted for fully 80 percent of national production. As the *National Glass Budget*, a trade publication, reminded its readers in 1921, "[I]t is desirable that the rest of the world should know — that the Pittsburg district is predominant in a number of industries. If we had no steel mills or electrical concerns, we might be known as the 'glass city'; for historically and also in point of the volume of our manufactures Pittsburgh has been the leader in the glass business."[5]

As new arenas opened in American life, as the urban landscape enlarged upwards and outwards, as humans charted the seas and explored the heavens, uses for the region's glass sky-

rocketed; windshields for automobiles, lighting for airport runways, night vision goggles, television tubes, and microchips — glass appeared in places never dreamed of. As the industry grew and expanded, researchers in development laboratories feverishly tried to imagine and then to invent new uses for glass or new types of glass.

PPG Place (the corporate headquarters of PPG Industries, Inc.) is a monument to glass that defines the modern skyline of downtown Pittsburgh. Yet, the city is better known as the "Steel City." The region and the country retain little consciousness of the pivotal role Pittsburgh played as the national center of production, innovation, and marketing for the glass industry.

While artifacts of the built environment — the glass cathedral of PPG, the stacks of factories now gone quiet — stand as silent reminders of a rich and complex past, audible reminders of that past are still heard in the region. Visit the industrial sites of the few independent producers, or the factories of the national and international conglomerates that still dot the landscape of Western Pennsylvania and the surrounding region; from their parking lots one can hear the roar and practically feel the heat of the furnaces. Step inside PPG Industries' factory in Meadville, Pennsylvania, for example, and the interplay of man, material, and machine unfolds — glass history being made today.

There is in glassmaking a sense of continuity with the past. The material is still formed using the same basic ingredients of sand, soda ash, and lime. The major means of production used in the past 200 years — blowing, pressing, and machine operations — are still employed. And the workforce is still largely white and male. Many of the products bear, in form or use, a resemblance to those of the past. What has changed most of all is where glass is or is not made. The region with Pittsburgh at its center, though still home to glass companies, no longer forms the core of the industry nationally.

A modern glass factory may introduce us to the past, but the products of the factory floor connect us most immediately to the story of glass. Each piece of glass made during the last two centuries was part of a process incorporating a functional or decorative concept or design with a system of production that included owners, workers,

Conical furnace stacks on this postcard identify the gritty mill site of Fort Pitt Glass Works, Jeannette, Pa., c. 1910.

and a site to house the tools and the machines for manufacturing. Equally important to the process was an economic system of market, demand, and sales, and a social and cultural context in which the glass object was used. The material objects provide an entry to the history of their manufacture, to the history of the place they were made, and to the lives of those who used them and saved them. This book is about the glass made in Western Pennsylvania, but it is also about the millions of people who bought, used, and collected that glass. The objects connect the threads of these composite stories; they represent and reflect American life and culture.

Most of us rarely think about the glass in our own lives, much less glass in the lives of those from the past. Perhaps this is partly because glass is usually transparent: we look through it, not at it. Yet, the physical property of transparency makes this miracle material desirable for a variety of uses and circumstances. Chemistry that allows for the clear or colorless property in glass means, of course, that glass can transmit light. The earliest products of the Western Pennsylvania region, window glass and bottles, were valued not only because they provided protection, but also because they were transparent. The word "window" itself denotes this: it comes from the roots *"vindr"* or "wind" and *"auga"* or "eye." Glass windows provide a protected view. Security window glass invented in the late 19th and early 20th centuries (wire glass and glass block) further capitalized on this property. They transmitted light — there was an element of transparency — but they were secure or stronger than regular flat glass. Transparency also made glass containers especially desirable in the early 20th century when the purity of food became a national public concern. Glass, non-porous and transparent, was perceived as a pure container. Glassmakers capitalized on this concern, marketing their wares with slogans such as, "Buy it in glass, see what you buy."[6]

The public/private dimension of glass has always been important to its structural and architectural applications. The Crystal Palace in London, built for the Great Exhibition of the Works of Industry of All Nations in 1851, represented a revolutionary use of glass in construction. This all-glass building with an iron skeleton demonstrated the ability of glass to bring

Above: "Carrying the Finished Plate," Pittsburgh Plate Glass Co., 1901. Below: The same qualities — transparency and reflectiveness — that made glass valuable for windows also made it ideal for elegant and decorative objects. The family history of this cut glass decanter (1823-1830) connects it to the Stourbridge Flint Glass Works.

Opposite page: While the Pittsburgh region was noted most for glassmaking, decorators such as Joseph Locke of Mt. Oliver also executed intricate acid-etched designs (goblet, c. 1910). Above: Glass workers sometimes fashioned chains to wear while marching in Labor Day parades. Albert C. Meyer, however, working at Glenshaw Glass just north of Pittsburgh, made this elaborate strand (c. 1920) for display in his home. Left: Consolidated Lamp & Glass turned out 400 dozen hand-painted lamps each day (this one c. 1905). Below: National Glass Co.'s 1904 catalog shows the daunting variety of Pittsburgh-area glassware.

the outside in, while the inside of a building is protected from exterior elements. One could see in from outside and out from inside. What fun and what marketing possibilities! With the ability to manufacture large sheets, or plates, of flat glass, this principle could be applied to department stores. Customers could preview wares without ever stepping inside and sales could be made from the sidewalk.

Glass can also be silvered or its surface coated so it becomes reflective, or more "private." In applications to eyeglasses, architecture, and automobiles, privacy glass ensures that the viewer sees out, but no one sees in. The optical properties of glass mean it can be bent or shaped so that it magnifies vision: worlds so private (small or far away) that they would never be visible to the naked eye are revealed through the use of glass.

Glass permeates worlds beyond the physical, imbuing objects made from it with powerful symbolic and contextual possibilities. Glass, a physical material, is also a verbal metaphor. In language, its physical properties (transparency, reflection, transmission of light and color, durability, and fragility) and physical forms have symbolic meaning.

Three-inch-long novelty glass shoes made by U.S. Glass Co. in Pittsburgh (c. 1900) with their reference to the "Cinderella" fairytale remind us that glass has meanings beyond the physical.

Glass exists in the metaphorical world as both a positive and a negative...

The glass may be half full or half empty.

A world of possibilities is glimpsed through a window of opportunity.

To achieve total understanding, things must be crystal clear.

Being overly optimistic is to see the world through rose-colored glasses.

Broken glass has symbolic meanings that share this dynamic of positive and negative. Mirrors and crystals both have a mystical association; they reflect truth and capture reality. A broken mirror represents seven years bad luck... yet broken toasting glasses seal a pact, preserving a moment forever. Christening a ship with a glass bottle is a similar act of commemoration. In this instance, it is the fragility of the glass container, the fact that it can be broken, that guarantees the success of the christening. The custom at Jewish weddings of the bridegroom stepping on a glass to mark the end of the ceremony is believed to recall the destruction of the temple in Jerusalem almost 2,000 years ago. Broken glass reminds us that the world is a fragile, sometimes terrible, place. That concept was immortalized in Germany on November 9 and 10, 1938, when Nazis terrorized the Jewish population, breaking into homes and destroying businesses. That terror is now known as "*Kristallnacht*" — "the night of broken glass."

This symbolic construct of glass as metaphor has also been used in literature and in popular culture. We understand implicitly the meaning of Cinderella's glass slipper; it represents truth and honesty because it is made of glass — it will only fit its rightful owner. Deceit in ownership would be signaled by the shattering of the slipper. The transparency or clarity of the slipper further enhances the object as a symbol of purity and truth — as the slipper slides on, its rightful owner is revealed for all to see.

So, too, with the mirror in *Sleeping Beauty*. In glass, especially the silvered glass of a mirror, the reflected image indicates the real. Mirrors, we all know, do not lie.

Glass is similarly used as a symbolic device in the movies and in television. It allows a glimpse of a private dimension, peeping through windows at night, or, when broken, signaling a seminal moment from which there is no turning back.

June Dunmire's collection of more than 1,000 creamers (late 19th century) documents the incredible variety of patterns available a century ago. Hand-decoration, ruby staining, gilding, or enamel painting provided even more choices.

Its physical qualities may be deployed as dramatic or symbolic devices.

Just as glass permits symbolic metaphors in language or literature or popular culture, so, too, may its physical attributes be assigned or inspire veneration. Beauty may be implicit in the object or imbued by the viewer; glass may be appreciated as fine art but also is often cherished or coveted for its symbolic meanings. Clearly the American public feels a special connection to the substance, as glass collectors form one of the largest group of collectors in the country. Many more people also identify with a single piece or group of objects that has special meaning to them alone. Glass given as a ceremonial gift for weddings or other celebrations, as a commemorative piece at proms or banquets, or purchased as a souvenir, is saved because it reminds one of a special event or place.

Glass also becomes infused with personality when it is passed person-to-person by those who share a relationship. The object's form and being are unchanged, but its value increases because it reminds one of the previous

For location of towns and factories in this chapter, see maps on page 158.

owner. Many collectors actively seek out that which they remember seeing or using — on grandmother's table, for instance, or in the cupboards of their childhood homes. Glass is sometimes saved by happenstance; it sits in the windows of old homes, or abandoned on telephone poles, or in the corner of the garage, or on a shelf in the basement. As often, it is saved or sought because of what it means to the seeker...

    or because the color calls us

    or because it is rare and beautiful

    or because it links us again to someone or someplace that matters.

In this way, glass frequently has value exceeding the sum cost of the ingredients and labor necessary to produce the piece. Value comes from the associations made with the object. Some associations, especially those of quality or rarity, make glass a valuable commodity. Both individuals and institutions seek to add to their collections that which is the best, or the only example of its type. Others collect because of the representative nature of the material, or because it tells a story rooted in people, place, and time. The Historical Society of Western Pennsylvania, for example, has built and preserved a collection of glass because of what it tells us about the region's past. Such glass links us to the people who invested in, and built, the industry; to names such as O'Hara, Ihmsen, Frank, Bakewell, Pears, Ford, and McKee that hung over the glasshouse doors; to men and women who took pride in their wares and saw the economic potential of the region. As Henry Clay Fry stated in 1901,

> There is room for another first class factory and another works will
> not injure the business. The country is growing, is rapidly increasing
> in wealth and people; more goods are constantly needed, especially
> good wares. I propose to demonstrate that the best and finest glass in
> the world can be produced here, and there is a market for still better
> things... I intend to start anew and produce a line of ware not now
> made in the country that will equal in every respect the fine crystal of
> Val St. Lambert or Baccarat.[7]

Glass also teaches us the names — Lee and Thomas, Hansen and Shaw, Schnupp and DeCrescenttis — who walked through the factory doors and created the objects. In addition, it connects us to the millions outside the region who bought and sold and used and saved the glass. The glass survives in the Historical Society's museum setting because of collectors, families, and museum staff who found it, claimed it, and brought it home to Pittsburgh, from whence it originally came.

Glass has import or meaning that ranges far beyond the regional confines of Western Pennsylvania. We share as a culture an understanding of how to use the products that were and are made in the region's factories. The products connect to a particular place, in a particular time, and the material serves as a starting place for understanding a system of manufacture and market. Use and shared understanding have created a cultural construct whereby the material is assigned symbolic meanings. By looking at the glass in our lives and in the past, we can begin to unlock those meanings.

The splendor of some glass objects makes the collector's impulse obvious. One example of exquisite design and craftsmanship is this covered bowl or "sweetmeat" (c. 1835) in the Midwestern hairpin pattern. Now in the collection of the Historical Society of Western Pennsylvania, it spent much of the last century in the hands of two notable glass collectors, William J. Elsholz and Walter E. Simmons, II.

CHAPTER 2

Beginnings

Opposite page: French illustrator Denis Diderot's (1713-1784) intricate engraving depicts the building of a glass furnace — the core of any glasshouse. Whether forming delicate goblets (right, possibly New Geneva Glass Works, 1800-1820) or blowing flat glass for windows, the early years of investment in the glass industry were mighty struggles for the region's entrepreneurs and artisans alike.

The year is 1803. Meriwether Lewis, trapped in Pittsburgh by the vagaries of a drunken boat-builder, is at last ready to set off on an adventure that will forever change the young nation. On August 31, with the Ohio River running low, Lewis steps into his Pittsburgh-built keelboat and heads west. The Lewis and Clark expedition is the talk of the countryside, the imagination of farmers and Washington politicians alike captivated by its possibilities. To the west lies land uncharted by European Americans — land which holds the potential for great commerce and development.

Albert Gallatin, a friend of President Jefferson and a statesman of national prominence from Western Pennsylvania, was well aware of the West's potential. An ardent map collector, Gallatin had special interest in the regions drained by the Missouri River. "The future destinies of the Missouri country,"

Gallatin stated, "are of vast importance to the U.S., it being perhaps the only large tract of country and certainly the *first* which lying out of the boundaries of the Union will be settled by the people of the U. States."[1] Gallatin had aided Lewis in his preparations for the expedition and even had a new map drawn for him that showed North America from the Mississippi River to the West Coast, blending the little-known about that region into one document. The hopes of many men rode off down the Ohio with Lewis on that August morning.

The population of Pittsburgh was especially attuned to the promise of the West. Sited at the confluence of the Allegheny, Monongahela, and Ohio rivers, the town's growth and development were linked to the inland water-ways. By 1803, the settled population was about 2,000, a number which swelled each spring as thousands of travellers streamed through on their way west. Pittsburgh was both a way station and a jumping-off point, a place to arrive at and a place to leave from.

Several travelers passing through in the early 19th century recorded their observations. Among them was Thomas Ashe, visiting in 1806, just three years after Lewis set off on his western travels. Ashe remarked:

Pale green glass was commonly used in the region for household products such as bowls (below, 1800-1840), as well as for window glass and bottles.

> No inland town in the United States, or perhaps in the world, can boast of a position superior to this... it being delightfully situated at the head of the Ohio, and on the point of land formed by the junction of the Alleghany and the Monongahela Rivers.... The spot on which this town stands, is so commanding (in the military phrase) that it has been emphatically called the key to the western country.... It contains about four hundred houses, many of them large and elegantly built with brick; and above two thousand inhabitants. It abounds with mechanics, who cultivate most of the different manufactures that are to be found in any other part of the United States; and possesses upward of forty retail stores, which all seem continually busy. To this place most of the goods conveyed in waggons over the mountains in spring and autumn, and destined for the Kentucky and Louisiana trade, are brought, to be ready for embarkation.[2]

In addition to its strategic location, Pittsburgh benefited from the geographical features of the region. The Allegheny Mountains made overland travel to and from cities on the Eastern Seabord arduous. In the early 19th century, the journey from Philadelphia to Pittsburgh was seven days in duration over rough, muddy roads. Travelers paid dearly for each household item or treasured piece of a former life they brought along. Freight costs and travel conditions made the shipping of fragile or heavy items especially prohibitive.

Even the well-to-do chose carefully when packing for the move across the mountains.

Pittsburgh, where the smoother highways of the inland river system began, became a busy marketplace for western-bound travelers. The town, however, was more than just a retailer of goods, for it was also a producer. The great seam of coal that sliced through the region provided fuel for nascent industry. By 1806, when Thomas Ashe visited, he could report, "Many valuable manufactures have been lately established here; among which are those of glass, nails, hats, and tobacco. The manufacture of glass is carried on extensively, and that article is made of an excellent quality."[3] Though not yet 10 years old, the region's glass industry was already worthy of note.

The two glasshouse partnerships established in the region during the 1790s were headed by entrepreneurs keenly aware of the region's potential. Albert Gallatin, a Swiss immigrant, first came to Western Pennsylvania in 1784 to examine a tract of land to which he had acquired title. He built a small log structure on his land in Fayette County at the junction of the Monongahela River and Georges Creek, a few miles south of present-day Masontown. Four years later, he purchased a nearby estate, Friendship Hill, and took it as his home. In the 1790s, Gallatin expanded his tract to encompass land lying on both sides of the mouth of Georges Creek. Though often away in Washington, D.C., he maintained and expanded his holdings on the edge of the frontier — in Western Pennsylvania and throughout the Ohio River Valley.

In 1795, Gallatin joined in partnership with his brother-in-law James Nicholson, and three other associates, John Badollet, Louis Bourdillon, and Charles Anthony Cazenove. The purchase by the five men of land near Gallatin's Fayette County holdings gave them access to the river system as well as proximity to the overland routes that linked Philadelphia, Baltimore, and the growing capital of Washington, with the West. The site, already home to three mills, seemed ripe for commercial development. The partners added a retail establishment and made efforts to establish a viable town, which they named New Geneva in honor of Gallatin's Swiss heritage.[4] Gallatin, fully realizing the commercial potential of the property, wrote to his wife:

> [W]e have the town seat (which is the nearest portage from the western waters to the Potowmack and the Federal City, and as near as any to Philadelphia and Baltimore) and three mill seats.... [T]he most valuable will be on the river-bank, so that we will be able to load boats for New Orleans from the mill-door, and they stand upon one of the best, if not the very best, stream of the whole country. The boat-yards fall also within our purchase, so that, with a good store, we will, in a

Albert Gallatin opened one of the area's first glasshouses, in Fayette County in 1797; though he knew nothing about glassmaking, Gallatin saw the potential for glass products in the developing West.

great degree, command the trade of this part of the country.[5]

The enterprise, known formally as Albert Gallatin & Co., was capitalized at $20,000 in an agreement that bound the partners for three years. Their business fortunes waxed and waned in the first two years, being severely tested in the second year by a general depression. In 1797, Gallatin's partners, intent upon initiating glass production in Western Pennsylvania, tried to persuade six German glassworkers at the New Bremen Glass Manufactory in Frederick, Maryland, to come to New Geneva instead of seeking their fortunes on the Kentucky frontier. Gallatin's partners were convinced that the tools were at hand for a successful business — fuel from forests they owned, plentiful sand from local rivers, and a market to the west hungry for glass.

Gallatin was less enthusiastic, believing that success and profits lay in the acquisition and development of real estate. He described the glass business as a "lottery ticket."[6] Eventually, however, he capitulated, and in September of 1797, an agreement was reached with five of the German glassblowers: George Kramer, Adolphus Eberhart, Lubowitz Reitz, Christian Kramer, and George Reppert. The Gallatin group paid to construct the glasshouse, and also covered operating expenses. Profits were to be split between the two groups, with the glassworkers also agreeing to reimburse the Gallatin group, without interest, for half of the start-up capital.

Correspondence between Gallatin, who was often away in Washington, and his partners documents the problems encountered by the fledgling glasshouse. Production troubles arose — in the proper curing of the wood used for fuel, in cleaning the sand, in preparing the batch, in procuring clay for the furnace pots — that sorely tested Gallatin's patience. In desperation, he instructed James Nicholson in March of 1798 to "rent or sell or abandon the works; but let us not melt everything we have in the attempt."[7] A reorganization of the business partnership resulted, with Gallatin buying out Badollet and Cazenove and splitting from Bourdillon. He retained ownership and control of the group's enterprises, with his brother-in-law Nicholson acting as his deputy. Gallatin also brought in a friend, a Mr. Mussard, to manage the glassworks and to remedy production problems. Matters seemed to improve and the group reported sales of £600.[8]

Forty-five miles to the north, in Pittsburgh, the O'Hara-Craig factory was encountering similar challenges. This partnership, too, had begun with great optimism. Isaac Craig reported in mid-1800:

Colonel O'Hara... as well as myself will be greatly obliged to you for assistance in procuring a man with the necessary qualifications of Foreman in a glass manufactory in which we have prospect of succeeding–the situation of our works being at least equal to any in the

James O'Hara, an Irish immigrant who rose to a colonel's rank in the Revolutionary War, was a partner in the Pittsburgh Glass Works, which opened the same year as Albert Gallatin's firm. A shrewd businessman, O'Hara made dark green or black porter bottles (opposite page, 1820-1860) for one of his other investments — a brewery. Bottles could be shipped more easily than kegs.

United States–being on the bank of the river at the foot of the Coal
Hill (opposite the Point Bridge) out of which we are supplied with
the best Coal I suppose in the world and at a trifling expence. The
principal component materials of Glass are also conveniently obtained
and our river a safe road of conveyance for brittle ware....[9]

James O'Hara, like Gallatin, was fully confident of the region's commercial potential. An Irish immigrant, he came to America in 1772 at the age of
20 and found employment as an agent trading with Native Americans. That
work brought him to Western Pennsylvania. It is believed that he began buying property in the region as early as 1773, eventually acquiring tracts across
a wide area into what is now Ohio, Indiana, and Illinois. O'Hara served as an
officer during the Revolution, marching his troops as far as Vincennes (now
in Indiana). In 1781, he was appointed assistant quartermaster, eventually
being stationed at Fort Pitt. Eleven years later, he was promoted to quartermaster general of the Army of the United States, a position which aided in his
development of business contacts in the West. O'Hara's business and military
careers were complementary: he traveled widely both overland and on the
rivers, developed networks of trade and commercial relationships, and
became an apt negotiator.

His first business venture involved the salt trade. O'Hara conceived of a
means to bring salt from a salt works in Salina, New York, that reduced costs
by half. Making the route from New York to Pittsburgh viable required
O'Hara to carry out a series of engineering improvements for river navigation,
as well as to build the boats and wagons for portage. Shortly thereafter,
O'Hara joined his fellow Pittsburgher Isaac Craig in establishing a glasshouse
at the foot of Coal Hill (now Mt. Washington) across the Monongahela River
from Pittsburgh. Available capital, business experience, and trade contacts not-
withstanding, the partners struggled with their new venture. While entrepre-
neurship often is advanced as a pivotal force on the frontier, exploring in
some detail the duo's obstacles and accomplishments reveals the complex
web of activities that fostered commercial development in the new republic.

For location of towns
and factories in this
chapter, see maps on
page 158.

Unlike Gallatin, O'Hara and Craig did not have an immediate source of
skilled glassworkers, and had to recruit them in the East and abroad. To bol-
ster recruitment efforts, O'Hara had worker housing built on the glasshouse
site. In correspondence, O'Hara mentions the new frame housing with space
for gardens available near his factory. In one letter describing his operations,
he explains his offer to skilled men of "dwelling houses and the best coal
fuel at their doors, all free from cost, and all travelling expenses paid from
their places of residence...."[10]

Worker housing also helped O'Hara and Craig's balance sheet, since part
of a worker's wages could be "paid" in the form of free or reduced-cost

housing. Such arrangements became commonplace once the glass industry began to expand in the early years of the 19th century. For example, workers at the Bakewell glass factory near downtown Pittsburgh, which after its founding in 1808 quickly earned an international reputation for leaded glass, clustered in housing around the manufactory in an area known as "Bakewell's Court."[11] Another glasshouse owner, George Hogg, who from 1827 until 1849 operated a glassworks in Brownsville, some 30 miles south of Pittsburgh on the Monongahela River, had three frame dwellings built on the property for workers. The two-story homes appear in a sketch of his works.[12]

At the Lorenz factory in west Pittsburgh and the McCully factory in south Pittsburgh, the city directory of 1856-57 neatly documents the addresses for glassworkers. From the directory, a fairly graphic picture of accommodations for early industrial workers may be drawn. Frederick Lorenz's factory succeeded glassmaking at the original O'Hara/Craig site, on what is now West Carson Street on the city's South Side, just below downtown's Point. In addition to the glassworks, Lorenz owned the lots extending up Coal Hill, probably for the mineral rights and not for development. Just east of the factory stood the Zug and Painter Iron Works, which had its own rows of worker housing. The city directory documents that glassworkers lived in a series of dwellings up to #49 in "Lorenz's Row." An 1830s deed suggests the "new frame houses erected by Mr. Lorenz" were made of wood.[13]

It is unknown how the homes were laid out, but primarily skilled workers (blowers and cutters), and office staff, such as clerks, lived in the dwellings with low numbers — 1 to 29. Although a few blowers are found in dwellings

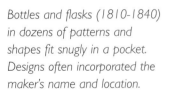

Bottles and flasks (1810-1840) in dozens of patterns and shapes fit snugly in a pocket. Designs often incorporated the maker's name and location.

numbered 30 to 49, laborers accounted for over 50 percent of the residents. This would seem to indicate some advantage to living in the dwellings with lower numbers; perhaps they were closer to the factory — or possibly further away, distance from the plant perhaps being preferable — or maybe the lower-numbered dwellings were large or in some other way more desirable. A variety store operated by Frederick Lorenz was located at 15 Lorenz's Row. Workers boarded at several of the dwellings and five widows also resided in the row with both Mary A. Lauth and Annie Rehr at #6. From the few workers who appear in the 1856-57 city directory and in either the 1850 or 1860 census, households appear to have contained only immediate or extended family, and most workers, usually married with children, were in their 20s or 30s. Some of their children were born in other states — primarily New Jersey, New York, and Maryland — where glass manufactories were located. Such birth patterns clearly indicate that skilled workers pursued opportunity, with one blower, David Edwards, moving in a three-year span from Pennsylvania to New York and then back again to Pennsylvania.[14]

This rare 1812-1813 report lists workers' output at the Pittsburgh Glass Works. In the era of artisanship, much of the work was done by hand; output and, ultimately, company profits depended on the workforce's training and skill.

Data on the McCully factory housing is not quite as complete, but it replicates some patterns evident in the Lorenz operation. The McCully complex was on Washington Pike, upriver from Lorenz's at the foot of the Monongahela Suspension Bridge (now known as the Smithfield Street Bridge) over the Monongahela River. Workers lived in two rows of housing, one of brick and the other of frame construction. Though listings exist for only about half the housing, a pattern does emerge. For the most part, skilled workers such as blowers, flatteners, and cutters lived in the brick housing and laborers lived in the frame dwellings. In the 1850s, it appears, class distinctions found on the factory floor persisted in housing as well.

Recruiting skilled workers and providing for their needs were just small parts of establishing a viable business. James O'Hara and Isaac Craig, for example, struggled to make the first Pittsburgh glasshouse a going concern. In 1804, Craig resigned from the partnership, with O'Hara buying out his shares, which amounted to about three-eighths of the business. After that date, O'Hara managed the business on his own, occasionally turning away the offers of men such as P.R. Frieze, a Baltimore merchant, to buy in as partners.[15] A great deal of O'Hara's time was spent managing the details of the business — recruiting workers, arranging for the shipment of raw materials, finding reputable sales agents, and collecting debts.

Even with coal literally at the glasshouse door, O'Hara labored to keep his works up and running. Securing the basic ingredients of production was a constant task. Local sand from the riverbeds was abundant, but as late as 1806, O'Hara explained to competitors to the south at New Geneva, "I send

From Sand to Substance

In 1998, an artisan in Delancey, N.Y.
(Art Reed of Sweetwater Glass),
reproduced an early blown pitcher
from the Historical Society's collection.
After gathering molten glass on the
end of his blowpipe, he shapes the
piece at his glassblower's bench.

Using tongs, the artisan gradually
shapes the glass.

2

1

The handle is applied as the
glass cools, changing color from
fiery red to yellow.

4

The neck and lip are formed,
though the glass remains very
hot and fluid.

3

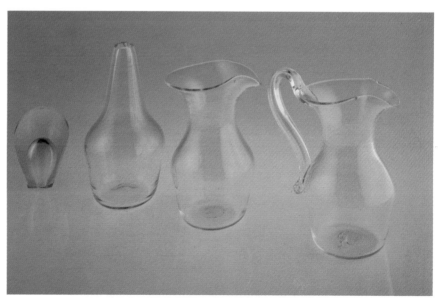

The four stages of production pictured together.

Mr. George Cochran to you for a sample of the Sand used at the Geneva Works, being informed that it is cleaner than the bank sand that I have been using."[16] When "cleaner" sand is melted — sand without trace minerals — untinted glass products are possible. In February of 1807, he sent a keelboat to retrieve sand from the river beds near Morgantown, in modern-day West Virginia.

As for necessary ash compounds, obtained from the burning of hardwood trees, demand was so great that O'Hara also purchased ash by wagonload from as far away as central Pennsylvania and upstate New York. During the War of 1812, two of O'Hara's shipments of ash were lost when British troops burned warehouses holding his shipments in Buffalo and Geneva, New York, costing him almost $1,000 in lost raw materials.[17]

During this time, glasshouse furnaces contained individual receptacles made of a formed and fired clay, called "pots," in which the batch of raw materials was melted. Locating clay that could withstand the intense heat of the furnace was a constant concern. O'Hara advertised in local papers offering a $100 reward to anyone discovering local stores of suitable clay. Primarily he purchased clay from afar — deposits of white clay in New Castle, Delaware, and Bordentown, New Jersey, and also imported from Germany. O'Hara's instructions to his shippers note his increasing familiarity with the technology of pot production. He cautions Mr. Labes, the merchant shipping him clay from Baltimore, to wait until April 1 to send his clay, to avoid any chance of it freezing. Several workers were employed just in the pot rooms and it appears their skills were greatly needed, as production records for the nine months of September 1812 to June 1813 document 131 pots broken during manufacture.

The primary articles of manufacture from O'Hara's glassworks, just as from Gallatin's, were window glass and hollowware. Settlement of the expanding nation meant construction of houses, businesses, churches, and institutions. Window glass brought light into the dark corners of new homes, extending the days and warming the body. Glass lights or panes, some as large as 13-by-18 inches, sheathed new shops, allowing a preview of the treasures within. Hollowware — glass bowls and pans, jugs and jars, bottles, flasks, tumblers, and decanters — provided the homemaker and shopkeeper with an indispensible, non-porous, utilitarian container for food preparation or storage. Glass also became a travelling companion — the bottle for the hip pocket — for countless Americans on their daily rounds. And it became the display item for salesmen seeking to entice shoppers into the stores. Transparent or darkest black, glass bottles and containers held equally well the promise and surprise to be found inside.

O'Hara offered both lines of ware to customers around the nation, with window glass seemingly more requested than the hollowware. In this period, window glass could be produced in two ways. In the crown method, a gob of molten glass was gathered at the end of a blowpipe, slightly inflated, and then cut open. It was then spun rapidly until it flattened. After the piece was "annealed," or slowly cooled, it was cut into panes. The center piece retained a bull's-eye or slightly thicker point from where the glass was attached to the metal rod. However, most window glass in Western Pennsylvania appears to have been produced using the cylinder method. O'Hara describes his glass in an 1811 letter as "...all the best cylinder glass I ever saw."[18] In this method, a cylinder was blown and shaped, and then was swung back and forth to elongate it. The cylinder was then scored and its ends removed before being gradually reheated. During reheating, it either slumped or was flattened with tools. After annealing, the piece was cut into finished panes.

Cutting of the panes was often a specialized task in the glasshouse. However, O'Hara's letters indicate that his blowers also became proficient cutters, giving them work when the furnaces were down. The cutting was done with diamonds, and in 1809 O'Hara searched for new bits, having used the original ones since 1798. "[Y]ou will confer a singular favor," he wrote to a merchant named Davidson in Washington, D.C., "by purchasing one dozen

The colors of this pan, inkwell, and pitcher (1800-1830) result from impurities or minerals in the sand. "Pure" sand for colorless glass sometimes came from Missouri or the East.

Opposite page: Benjamin
Bakewell presented this decanter
(c. 1845), according to family
history, to Ellen Murdoch —
establishing the famous
Pittsburgh factory's engraved
"daisy and leaf" pattern.

or as many new diamonds as you can under that number and send[ing] them by mail. I cannot go on without them."[19] Panes were made in a variety of sizes. Studying orders, it seems the best seller was an 8-by-10 inch "light" (the other term for a pane). Several times, O'Hara laments that size being out of stock, and once in 1806, he even refers an order he was unable to fill to Gallatin in New Geneva.

The most prized worker in the window glasshouse was the master blower or "gaffer." The factory was generally organized into shops with a master craftsman at the head, assisted by journeymen workers, apprentices, and sometimes non-indentured boys. The apprentice often did the gathering, taking up the molten glass from the furnace pots and then sometimes shaping it on the "marver," or table, before it was delivered to the blower. The blower inflated and shaped the glass, often working at the bench or chair. If the piece needed an applied collar or lip (in the case of a bottle), or a foot or a handle (as with tableware), the blower would work those operations at the bench. The apprentice then helped remove the piece from the blowpipe and carried it to the annealing ovens, where it was slowly cooled to temper the piece and prevent breakage.

At any point, the boys in the glasshouse might offer assistance, sweeping up, stoking the furnace, providing tools to the workers. Journeymen had the skills do some blowing, as well as other tasks, but were not as accomplished or as quick as a master craftsman.

The monetary value of the master craftsman is attested to by a production report from the O'Hara works. Charles Imsen (possibly "Ihmsen"), working two pots over nine months in 1812-13, delivered to the O'Hara warehouse 329 boxes of window glass. (A box contained 100 square feet of glass.) In the same period, he also blew 8,500 quart and porter (beer) bottles. A less skilled, possibly journeyman blower, John Hane, working one pot during the same nine months, made only about one-third the window glass (91 3/8ths boxes and 3,550 bottles). O'Hara paid his master craftsmen about $100 cash a month, plus lodging and free heating coal. With window glass selling at $13 a box, O'Hara grossed about $3,400 from the output of a single skilled worker like Imsen. The glass business had the potential to be quite profitable.[20]

The market for Western Pennsylvania window glass and hollowware was extensive. It seems logical that O'Hara was himself a customer, requiring porter bottles to hold the product of his brewery, the Pittsburgh Point Brewery. He shipped window glass near and far, to Bedford and Chambersburg in Pennsylvania, and to cities from Ohio to New York. His glass went downriver to Lexington, St. Louis, Natchez, and New Orleans, and

east and south over the mountains to Baltimore, Philadelphia, and Charleston. His bottles, too, traveled far and wide. While sending a Mr. William Morris of Carlisle an order of window glass in 1809, O'Hara slipped in a price sheet for his hollowware: "I have annexed the prices of my hollow glass would this article do with you. I pack it in cases of $20 value weighing about 100 pounds."[21]

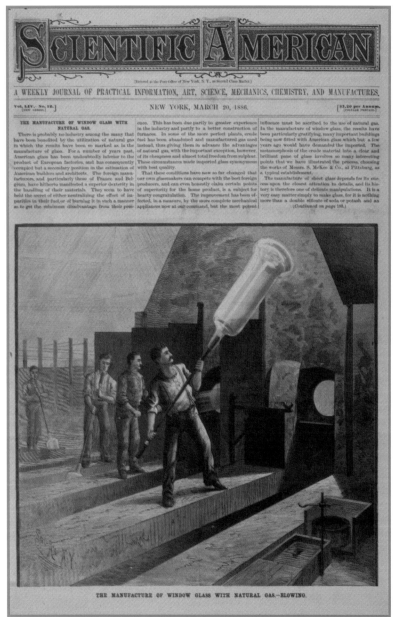

THE MANUFACTURE OF WINDOW GLASS WITH NATURAL GAS.—BLOWING.

While O'Hara's wares found a ready market, his retailers were not always prompt in holding up their end of the deal. In a series of letters in 1811, he endeavored to collect the "many balances due the glass works" that had exhausted his capital reserves.[22] Bills for glass to be sold on commission or credit were as much as two or three years overdue. His quality was undoubtedly high, and he bragged that his glass sent to Philadelphia had been judged a superior product by merchants there, as good as any but the finest New England glass. It wasn't that his glass didn't sell, O'Hara believed, but that his retailers did not pay.

By 1810, O'Hara also faced increased competition for the domestic market. The industry had expanded in Pittsburgh, as well as in New England and throughout the Mid-Atlantic states. Other entrepreneurs recognized the potential profits to be made, with an expanding national market and improving transportation for reaching that market. The federal census of that year recorded 10 window glass manufactories in business employing about 140 glassblowers and producing 2.7 million square feet of glass. This production was exactly one-half the market, with an equal amount of imported window glass filling the void. One Boston works provided a crown window glass described as "equal to any imported," while other works made green or German (probably cylinder) glass.

Domestic production of hollowware and bottles was also expanding, and two recently established works in Pittsburgh supplied "decanters, tumblers, and every other description of flint glass of a superior quality."[23]

One of the most prominent flint (leaded) glass houses, as noted earlier, started as Benjamin Bakewell & Co. This firm still enjoys a reputation as one of the best-known and most-revered of the Pittsburgh factories, though it has been out of business since 1882. An insurance description from August 19, 1808, indicates that the glasshouse was completed and in operation by that date.[24] The lot fronted the Monongahela River along Water Street, a central location with easy access to downtown Pittsburgh and the river. Like O'Hara and Gallatin, the company's production lines included bottles and window glass, but Bakewell was best known for its colorless glass.

Thomas and Benjamin Bakewell and their associate Benjamin Page brought capital and business acumen to the partnership, while for glass expertise they relied on workers such as Edward Ensell. As early as April 1809, the company advertised an "assortment of products," which, as detailed in later ads, included decanters of three types, tumblers, goblets, wine glasses, jars, tinctures, lamps, butter and sugar "basens," cream jugs, wine coolers, egg cups, and on and on.[25] The firm was visited by the well-known and unknown alike, and numerous accounts of its operations found their way into print. Of note are the positive comments on the cold processes of decoration executed at the firm, namely cutting and engraving. "I went through the flint glass works of Mr. Bakewell," remarked one Thomas Nuttal in 1819, "and was surprised to see the beauty of this manufacture, ... in which the expensive decorations of cutting and engraving ... were carried to such perfection."[26] Of the glass made for President Andrew Jackson, it was said: "We think this specimen of American workmanship will vie with the best productions of the French and British articles."[27] Glowing reports abound. By the late 1810s, Bakewell clearly had established a reputation for quality and workmanship that attracted an enviable clientele, including the White House.

The Bakewell factory is also recognized as the training ground for the second generation of glasshouse owners in Pittsburgh. Men whose names would later be associated with their own major concerns — Thomas Evans, William McCully, James Bryce, and others — began their careers at Bakewell. Following the fortunes of one of these families demonstrates the important role that Bakewell played in furthering Pittsburgh's industry; the exercise also exposes the sometimes brutal workplace arrangements of the early 19th century.

The Bryces were Scottish immigrants who came to Pittsburgh from Philadelphia in 1820. A young son, James, his father, and older brother William found work as common laborers at Bakewell, the father then advancing to the manufacture of lead, which probably contributed to his early death a year or two later. The family was poor and James' career at the glasshouse

The prominent jowls of Pittsburgher Edward Dithridge (portrait, c.1865) attest to his career as a glassblower. Starting as an apprentice in the 1830s, he rose to head the Fort Pitt Glass Works. Opposite page: The making of window glass before machine technology is depicted in this 1886 image. Craftsmen, heating glass attached to a blowpipe, created cylinders reaching 8 feet long. Cylinders were then down the middle, reheated, and flattened before being cut to size.

had begun at age 11. He describes himself as the "youngest boy about the place," proud to bring home his dollar and a quarter each Friday night to contribute to the family accounts. He worked directly for a blower, probably as a carrying boy, for he reports being "there nearly two years before I began to gather." Work was hard and long and James bore the brunt of a brutal master, recording his treatment with scant attention to literary convention:

> He never beat me because he could find no reasonable excuse to do so. but he made me miserable by a continual system of petty annoyance and vexation and scolding and swearing at me .... After I left him he wished me to go back to work for him again. I refused, and from that time he became my bitter enemy using every means in his power to injure me. and even, with forecasting malice trying to hinder me from learning my trade. by falsehoods to the masters. as well as by endeavoring to destroy what little confidence I had in myself. but let it pass, I had the satisfaction of knowing him thoroughly and despising him heartily.[28]

In 1826, James' father lay dying. On his death bed, he asked the Bakewell firm to apprentice his son. Within the year, James would sign a formal indenture to apprentice as a glassblower and learn the "art, trade, and mystery" of glass.[29] He began his career in the "smalls" department, where wine glasses, salts, cream jugs, and other table items were produced. He then progressed to working in the castor pots. He both came of age and completed his apprenticeship in 1833, but it was not until two years later, when the blower H. Whitehouse left, that he was offered a place as a master blower. James Bryce, age 23, had already spent 12 years in the glasshouse, yet was ambiva-

Flint Glass Manufactory.

BAKEWELL & ENSELL,

INFORM their friends and the public in general, that they have now on hand, and offer for sale, at their Flint Glass Manufactory, in Pittsburgh, a complete assortment of the following articles, viz.—

Quart and pint Decanters,
Half pint and gill do.
Quart and pint Tumblers,
Half pint and gill do.
Cream Jugs and Sugar Basins,
Pocket Flasks, Salts,
Phials, Proof Bottles, &c. &c.

Merchants from the states of Ohio, Kentucky, Tennessee. &c. will find their advantage in sending for their supplies as early as possible

All orders will be duly attended to and faithfully executed.

Pittsburgh, Oct. 19, 1808.

N. B. Cash given for Pot and Pearl Ashes.

Top: Just a few months after opening in 1808, Bakewell & Ensell advertised a broad range of wares to merchants in the Ohio River Valley. Right: Tumblers engraved with greyhounds (c. 1825) captured the admiration of visitors to the Bakewell factory; Benjamin Bakewell gave the glass on the left as a gift to John Reynolds.

lent about "the place I hold now," a station in life that once was "the bound of my ambition but now when it is attained it gives me little pleasure."[30]

As James struggled on the factory floor to chart his future and determine his fate, so too did the Bakewells and all American glassmen struggle in the 1820s and '30s to navigate the ever-changing currents of their business. National economic conditions and international political realities buffeted the market. The American glass business had expanded during the boom years of the War of 1812, when an embargo on imported goods had benefited the nation's manufacturers by protecting them from cheaper foreign glass. As Benjamin Page recalled later in a letter:

> [I]n the year 1813... we were then at war with England & by the tone of the communications of our Executive to the citizens of America — as well as by the feeling prevalent in the country & cherished by the Government, every body believed the prospect of peace was distant.... The demand for glass increasing rapidly in consequence of the restrictions on foreign importations of the article, induced us to exert ourselves to the utmost to 'make hay while the sun shone' — and when peace was restored in 1814 bringing the full tide of successful experience as Mr. Jefferson would express it we prosecuted the business with the greatest possible vigour not doubting the result would be singularly prosperous....[31]

While pressure from imports was extinguished, glass manufacturers had also begun to enjoy unprecedented access to the nation's western markets. Innovations in transportation, especially the introduction of the steamboat to western waters in 1811, made the movement of goods cheaper and easier.

Pittsburgher James Lee designed and blew these delicate tumblers (c.1835) as a betrothal gift for his fiancée Charlotte Barker. The rose signifies her English ancestry — the thistle his Scottish heritage.

Several owners, O'Hara and Gallatin among them, recognized the value of better transportation, of all kinds, to the successful prosecution of business. They advocated public management and improvement of both roads and waterways, and the linking of the two to create a more unified system. Canals and bridges, they could see, speeded commerce.

O'Hara had seen the benefits first-hand when he reworked the transport routes from upstate New York to Pittsburgh to slash the price of salt (an essential frontier commodity for preserving and curing). Albert Gallatin, meanwhile, travelled often between Friendship Hill and the nation's capital, giving him long personal experience with the awful state of the roads. He further recognized that the country's new markets lay principally to the west, and that being able to reach and develop the interior of the country would require drastic improvements in all systems of transportation known at the time. A substantial percentage of Gallatin's writings and speeches before Congress was devoted to extolling how travel made easier would multiply the "national wealth."

In response, the national government did embrace the cause of infrastructure-building, supporting the building of national roads and turnpikes, as well as canals. Pennsylvania also allocated massive financing for transportation in the first half of the 19th century. Of the 2,333 corporations chartered in Pennsylvania between 1790 and 1860, two-thirds were transportation companies. The state purchased more than $100 million worth of shares in canal and railroad companies during that period. Pittsburgh, in the western corner of the state, was more often than not the western terminus of state-financed improvements.[32]

Americans enjoyed a brief respite from European, especially British, com-

Top: Many sugar bowls (1825-1850) are attributed to Bakewell, though other area factories also made purple glass objects. Right: The steamboat's coming to the U.S. interior after the War of 1812 improved trade and travel, but also opened river markets to British competitors.

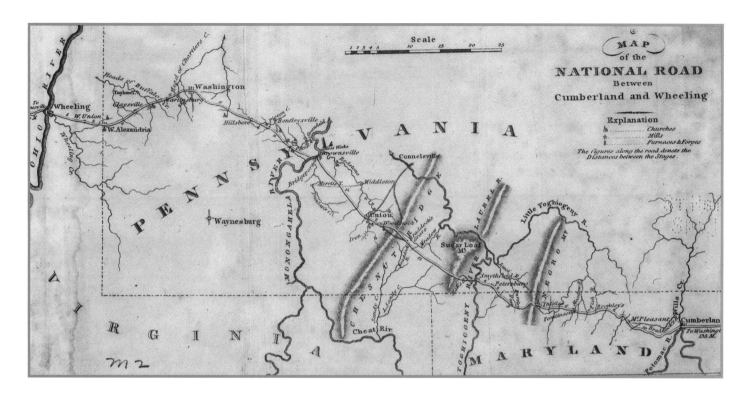

petition after peace in the War of 1812 was declared in 1814. President
Madison, aware of the beneficial effects of embargo on his nation's manufacturers, retained wartime duties on imports for two more years. During the
keelboat days, before the war and the steamboat, when products could be
moved most economically downstream, Pittsburgh glasshouse owners had
been better positioned than Europeans to exploit the western markets. After
the war, however, in 1816, with the steamboat allowing cheaper movement of
goods to the nation's interior — upstream as well as downstream for
the first time, via the port of New Orleans and the inland river system — the British began exporting huge volumes of glass. Having
made glass for 400 years, they had remedied the production
problems still shackling American manufacturers, and had a
pool of skilled workers from which to draw. British producers
devastated many American glassmakers, including those in
western Pennsylvania.

In addition, domestic competitors to Pittsburgh glass
improved their positions when one of the modernizations that
Gallatin and O'Hara had begged for — the National Road (present-
day U.S. 40) — opened in 1818, connecting both Mid-Atlantic and
western cities with Pittsburgh. As other improvements in roads, bridges, and
canals became operative in the 1820s, Pittsburgh's glassmakers found themselves throttled on all fronts.

The 1820 U.S. Census of Manufactures records in detail complaints of

Top: The National Road, the nation's first major publicly funded highway, ignited trade and travel through the region. Improving transportation networks ranked high on the list of priorities that glassmen Gallatin and O'Hara believed vital for their industry's success. Left: A champion of the National Road and of federal tariffs to protect U.S. industries in the early 19th century was the well-known politician Henry Clay.

Right: Travel on the nation's roads and rivers, as this 1830s cartoon depicts, was wild and risky for glass companies trying to market and distribute goods in the West. Bottom: Note the elegant vertical ribbing and the rich color of this blown cruet, c. 1830.

local factory owners. From Fayette County: "[T]his institution would be in a flourishing condition — the sale & demand for the articles rapid & Extensive, but for the immense importations of Glass from Europe." Across the river from Pittsburgh, meanwhile, a window and hollowware manufacturer reported how imports drove down prices: "[A] Box of Glass would sell for $14 Cash when at the present time a Box cannot command In Trade more than $5 — If the demand for Glass does not increase all such Establishments must Shut up." Finally, the report from the esteemed Bakewell of Pittsburgh recounted in detail the difficulties facing glass manufacturers. The firm's use of raw materials had plummeted from the 80-100 tons of 1815, a boom year, to 20 tons in 1820. In the same period, the workforce shrank from 30 men and 30 boys earning about $20,000 to 10 men and 12 boys earning about $6,000. The value of the company's manufactured product had fallen by four-fifths, to about $20,000. Bakewell summarized the situation in clear terms for the government:

Since the year 1816 the establishment has been declining — partly owing to the embarrassed situation of the Western merchants — but chiefly to the incessent importation of foreign glass and the sales of it at auction much below its intrinsic value. The import (tax) on glass is at present less than it was 15 or 20 years ago[.] It is introduced into our markets by means of Steam Boats at less than one fourth of the former expence of transportation from the Seaboard — & the late allowance of bounty paid by the British Government on Glass exported to the United States is more than the amount of duty on Importation. To these causes combined is attributed the extreme depression of our business — and until they are removed, at least partially, no improvement in the demand for the articles of our manufacture can be expected.[33]

Benjamin Page, describing the desperation many businessmen felt, lamented that "from the beginning of 1817 till about the middle of 1822 we were literally gasping for breath — & often knew not from Tuesday to Friday & again from Friday to Tuesday how we should get money to support our workmen." By 1818, the Bakewell firm owed $50,552 and carried an additional $37,960 in accounts due that Page described as "very doubtful."[34] The firm, which provided elegant cut decanters for President Madison in 1816 and was at work in November 1818 on glass for President Monroe, was in an "appalling situation."[35] All the manufacturers in the city of Pittsburgh felt the awful pinch, as employed workers in the city and vicinity decreased from 1,960 to 672 between 1815 and 1819. In the glass industry, in December 1819, the depression was evident: glassworks and glass cutting workers had fallen from 169 to 40; product value from $235,000 to $35,000.[36]

Storekeepers used glass jars (1835-1875) to showcase bulk foods or goods. Popular, such jars were made locally until the late 19th century.

By this time, it was clear that the country's economic future lay to the west. Yet, even those areas faced desperate economic conditions during the period, further handicapping U.S. manufacturers intent on expansion. As with transportation, the national government intervened. Spokesmen for Western Pennsylvania manufacturers were both politicians attuned to their concerns, such as Henry Baldwin, and men with national interests and reputations, such as Henry Clay. The two led the battle to enact a series of domestic tariffs in the 1810s and 1820s that provided a more favorable business environment.

In 1818, Baldwin, as chairman of the U.S. House Committee of Manufacturers, spearheaded passage of a duty increase on cut glass. The bill provided some protection for flint glass manufacturers such as Bakewell, but did little to help makers of window and container glass. Six years later, in 1824, with the support of protectionists such as Clay, a more comprehensive tariff known as "The American System" passed Congress. It incorporated not only Clay's desire to shield U.S. manufacturers but also permitted the country to earn a measure of commercial independence from England. "The truth is, and it is vain to disguise it," Clay had declared in 1820, "that we are a sort of independent colony of England — politically free, commercially slaves."[37]

The law was designed not only to provide a more fair international market for American goods, but also to develop the home market. Clay and many others believed that a strong manufacturing sector also provided a ready market for American farmers; those whose daily work was in the factory, the reasoning went, would rely on those whose work was on the farm, and vice-versa. The tariff had the desired effect. By January 1825, Benjamin Page reported, "The country certainly is rising from the depression and oppression to which it has been subjected for so long a time."[38] Although the tariff issue was not finally resolved — it would be revisited in the 1830s and again in 1842 — clearly government and industry had joined their interests.

In a little more than a quarter-century, great change had swept through the glass industry. Its owners and craftsmen wrestled locally with establishing and supplying the industry, while also involving themselves in issues of national import: building infrastructure, working with the federal government to stabilize the fledgling industry, and staking out the domain of technical expertise in which American manufacturing would excel. From two factories in 1797, the glass industry had expanded in Western Pennsylvania to include four factories in the city of Pittsburgh and five more in the surrounding region, with a total output valued at almost $200,000 a year. The 1826 city directory reported:

> In the manufacture of this article, Pittsburgh and the surrounding country, enjoys an extensive reputation. It is needless for us to repeat what we have said before, as to the advantages we possess — let it suffice, when we say, that the west, at least this part of it, is secure against any competition elsewhere in this branch of business. The glass of Pittsburgh and the parts adjacent is known and sold from Maine to New Orleans.... Should the waters of the east and west ever be connected, glass, of itself, will be an object of immense trade.[39]

Entrepreneurs such as Albert Gallatin, James O'Hara, the Bakewells, Benjamin Page, and hundreds of glass artisans such as Charles Imsen, James Bryce, and many others who remain nameless, are the progenitors in Western Pennsylvania glass history. Pittsburgh's commanding location and the region's abundance of natural resources — its coal, wood, and rivers — spurred industrialization on an ambitious scale. The technological change that is always a key part of commercial development would have a new focus in coming decades. Technology would reorder the factory floor; indeed, factories would grow to become huge complexes, and be reconfigured again and again. Technology, in fact, would do much more: it would also recast the glass marketplace.

Several local companies made cut glass. This compote (c. 1845) came from the South Side firm of Patrick Mulvany and James Ledlie. The company advertised its products as "cut, moulded and plain flint glassware."

SHATTERING
NOTIONS

Workshops

Pittsburgh was the nation's glass workshop during much of the 19th century. Firms clustered on the city's South Side included Cunningham & Ihmsen (opposite page, c. 1870). Glass employment and economic impact rivaled the metal trades, for which Pittsburgh is famous. Workers were mainly men, though women specialized in painting and decorating objects such as the exquisite vase, right, of Pittsburgh Lamp Brass, & Glass Co.

Textile factories and iron foundries, salt and shoe works, rolling mills and sawmills, steam engines and smokestacks — the landscape of Pittsburgh vibrated with the sights and sounds and smells of industry. With people bustling, and machinery and man humming in concert, there was activity everywhere. Nuggets of black gold fired the furnaces, great volumes of black smoke belched into the sky. Pumps and pistons, spindles and stacks, rabs and rollers — workforces on factory floors orchestrated a syncopated dance of coal-fired, steam-driven machinery. This was the city at work, Pittsburgh, the Birmingham of America:

Ascend the hill around which the city lies and you may see hundreds of furnaces vomiting forth immense volumes of black smoke mingled with red flames. Among them are scattered

A pane of window glass by Bakewell, Pears & Co. (c. 1840) has the all-over design collectors call "lacy," which hid imperfections created in the molding process. Below: Three pieces from the 1830s show how hand work and mold patterns were joined in the factory: the bowl on the far left uses the same pattern as the bowl on the right, which has a base identical to the pattern on the cup plate, center.

little steam pipes peeping from the roofs & always snorting out their white steam like so many whales. There are foundries & glass houses & salt works & steam mills & steam factories without number... so full is the city of smoke from all these immense fires of mineral coal that one cannot see from one end of a straight level street to the other. The coal is dug as free as dirt all over the country for fifty miles around.[1]

It was in this milieu that the glass industry came of age in the middle decades of the 19th century. Throngs of mechanics and machinists contributed greatly to a culture where commerce and industry were of one consciousness. A place where the intellectual capital of industry would prove as important as the material capital it generated, Pittsburgh would become the glass capital of the nation.

Once the nation's and the region's economy cleared the post-war crises of the 1810s and early 1820s, factory owners, able to rely as always on the country's rich supplies of natural resources, could concentrate on organizing human and technical capacity to meet the demand for glass objects. In the early 1820s, the methods for producing glass in Western Pennsylvania were little different from those used elsewhere for hundreds of years. The factory floor was organized into shops with master craftsmen at the head, tools were simple iron and wooden forms — the blowpipe, shears, jacks, and punty iron, allied with the carved wooden molds for shaping and patterning the blown glass — and the factory building and the furnaces were of a set and relatively simple design. By no later than 1826, however, change was afoot.

An American innovation, the mechanical pressing of glass, would revolution-
ize the industry.

It has long been thought that Pittsburgh's Bakewell company deserves the
greatest credit for the innovation of pressed glass. As furniture knobs were
the initial items known to be pressed, and a patent filed by John P. Bakewell
on September 9, 1825, is known to have claimed an "improvement in making
glass furniture knobs," Bakewell was assumed to have developed the
pressing process. But because all U.S. patents between 1790 and
1836 were destroyed by fire, the original Bakewell patent has
not been available to scholars. However, recent scholarship
indicates that pressing was first explicitly described and
patented by Henry Whitney and Enoch Robinson of the
New England Glass Co. on November 4, 1826.[2]

Previous to the Whitney-Robinson patent, small glass
objects such as furniture knobs and chandelier drops
could be pinched in simple hand-held presses or made
using a hand-held plunger to force molten glass into a mold.
In addition, pattern had been added to the surface of glass
objects for years by blowing the object into a carved, sometimes
hinged mold. However, the new mechanical process used a bench
press, a machine with a levered arm that could force the plunger or die into
the mold. The machine allowed for greater control of the pressing process

*Above: A protective
wooden mask (c. 1930)
called a "cowboard"
(probably because they
were usually made of
leather) was used widely in
the industry for several
decades; it was worn over
the face while checking
furnaces or gathering glass.
Left: Mold-makers devel-
oped highly detailed
patterns; note the fanciful
stems and intricate designs
on these glass lamps made
in the region during the
1870s.*

and standardized the decorative ornamentation of the glass piece.

Pittsburgh factories moved quickly to capitalize on this invention after John Robinson of the Stourbridge Flint Glass Works filed a patent in October of 1827 for pressed glass knobs. Bakewell filed again in May of 1828 for "an improved method of making glass furniture knobs or handles." Across America, glass companies joined the fray: at least nine patents for pressing glass were filed by the close of 1830, and an additional 24 patents were issued by 1836.[3]

It is not surprising that men such as the Bakewells recognized the potential of this new technology. They travelled widely throughout the Ohio River Valley investigating a variety of investment opportunities (oil wells in

A press machine used at the L.E. Smith Glass Co., Mt. Pleasant, Pa. The levered arm operated a plunger, which, when pulled down, forced a molten gob of glass against the sides of a carved mold.

Cincinnati and sawmills in Kentucky, to name just two). They witnessed first-hand fledgling industry and the steam-driven, interlocking metal machinery that powered it. As travellers made it a habit to tour the fiery mills of Pittsburgh, it seems safe to suppose that native Pittsburghers often crossed the thresholds of their fellow industrialists. The Bakewells, like many Pittsburgh business owners, involved themselves in the civic life of the city. Thomas Bakewell, who served appropriately enough as "Inspector of Pot and Pearl Ashes," as well as serving on bank and insurance company boards and as president of the Board of Trade shortly after its 1836 establishment, had cause to visit the city's business and commercial establishments. A great deal of useful information on industry, machinery, and manufacturing would have been available to a man in his position. Indeed, in the patent for a press machine filed by Thomas and John P. Bakewell on January 14, 1829, they described the design of this new glass press as "very similar to several of the modern printing presses, to many seal presses, working with the toggle joint, and various other machines."[4]

While pressing changed the production possibilities of the glass factory, it did not immediately affect the types or forms of glass made. Molded glass continued to replicate known forms, such as plates, bowls, salts, and other pieces of tableware. The advantage of pressing was speed and standardization: exact copies of the same object could be turned out by a pressing crew at a faster rate than if done by hand and each piece would look markedly alike. Deming Jarves of the Boston and Sandwich Glass Co. reported that a crew of five working a press could make "a beautiful tumbler in about forty seconds, or about one hundred in an hour," reducing the cost so much that by 1846, Jarves estimated that public demand for glass had increased tenfold.[5]

While not changing the product — except to standardize it — the press did force a reorganization of the factory floor. A press shop generally required the services of at least three workers. The pressing machine, with a mold in place, was set near the furnace. The first worker, usually a boy, gathered the glass from the furnace on a metal rod, called a punty. The gatherer held the taffy-like molten glass over the mold and the presser cut off the exact amount of glass needed for the piece with large scissor-like shears. The glass fell into the mold and the plunger was pressed down into it, forcing the glass up against the sides of the mold. After the glass had cooled slightly, a third worker opened the mold, removed the piece and carried it to the annealing oven. If the shop had multiple molds for the same piece and was working them continuously, one worker removed the piece from the mold and another, often a boy, carried the finished pieces to the annealing oven. The technology of molding pieces with handles did not develop immediately, so hand-finishing of pitchers, mugs, etc., was still done. In general, however, those shops that were press shops no longer relied on the master craftsman or skilled hot glass worker. The primary skilled workers were those who understood the interaction of hot glass and machinery: the presser, who did not hand-form objects but still had to possess hand/eye coordination and manual skills; and the mold-maker, who created and carved the metal molds in which glass was formed.

Of paramount concern when working with a mold made of iron or brass was maintaining its temperature. If it were too cold, the glass would stick to it, ruining the piece and slowing down the production schedule. If the temperature wavered, pitting and rough edges resulted. Pressed glass patterns were designed to disguise the imperfections caused by this interaction between the glass and the mold. Designs tended to cover the entire body of

Above: Many tools used in the glass industry have changed little in the last 100 years. A paddle and tongs (c. 1975) from Westmoreland Glass most likely were used to carry finished objects to the cooling ovens. Bottom: Notice in this 1871 image of making cylinder window glass the prevalence of child laborers and also the cowboards around the workers' necks.

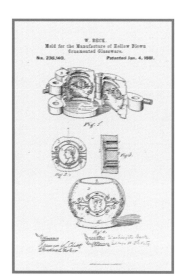

An 1881 patent drawing by a prominent Pittsburgh machinist and mold-makers maker, Washington Beck, explains the operation of his carved metal mold.

the piece, and backgrounds were filled with stippling. The early pressed glass of this type is known popularly to collectors as "lacy," because the all-over design often resembles delicate lace patterns. The intricate and time-consuming nature of the carving done to produce the molds for this glass may explain why most of the early pressed pieces were open bowls or flat pieces such as plates or window panes.

Mold-making was detailed work. Even in the early 20th century, when machinery and tools had been greatly improved, a single mold might take several hundred hours to complete, depending on the complexity of the piece.[6] Mold work was probably initially done by the blacksmiths who produced the metal tools for the glasshouse. Fairly soon after the invention of pressing, glass factories included mold-makers or machinists on staff. Independent mold shops also were established, with the shop of Pittsburgh mold-maker Joshua Laird in business by the late 1820s.[7] Molds were provided both for tableware and for bottle manufacturing, where the use of two-piece hinged metal molds was in widespread use by the 1830s. (All bottles were still blown into molds, their narrow necks making mechanical plungers unworkable.)

Improved national economic conditions, the invention of pressing, and the growth of a national market that could afford glass products — now less expensive than ever — led to rapid expansion of the industry. By 1840, there were 28 glass factories in Western Pennsylvania; 15 were in Pittsburgh and its immediate environs, and the other 13 were in Washington and Fayette counties. The region was home to one-third of the nation's glass producers, and its output was valued at 24 percent of the national total, which was $702,000.[8]

Industry expansion based on pressed glass technology increased demand for skilled machinists and mold-makers. A preeminent national mold shop, Washington Beck's, opened in Birmingham (Pittsburgh's South Side) in 1859. Beck's skills and enterprises were wide-ranging: his firm designed and produced molds, presses and machinery; he patented glass production methods, machinery and designs; he was a silent partner in glasshouse ventures; and he was a founder of South Side's Iron and Glass Bank. From a small room of just 8-by-12 feet, his business grew to fill a two-story building of 72-by-80 feet with 30 workers. By 1886, his products were in use throughout America, and in Europe and Japan.[9]

In the decades after the Civil War, as the region's glass industry burgeoned, so, too, did independent mold shops. In 1856, a number of such machinists appeared in the Pittsburgh directories, some like Marshall & Brothers doubtless serving the glass industry as they included among their products hand and lever presses. Washington Beck was the first to list his shop as a mold-making business and to mention specifically glass molds and presses in his advertisements. By 1880, three companies advertised as producers of glass molds and presses, and one, the Pittsburgh Clay Pot Co., as a specialty producer of glass melting pots. By 1885, 12 companies just in Pittsburgh provided pots, presses, molds, and glass production materials such as sand. There was significant integration of capital between the glass industry and its support industries. For instance, the Diamond Alkali Co. was founded by the directors of the Macbeth-Evans Glass Co. in concert with glassmaker C.L. Flaccus and the Hazel Atlas Glass Co. Their investment guaranteed ready access to soda ash and other chemicals for glassmaking without going through an outside supplier.[10] As Western Pennsylvania became the center for glass production, support industries providing machinery, tools, and materials flourished.[11]

A combination of other factors also spurred growth. An innovation in the chemical formula for glass was of central importance to the expansion, for instance, of the pressed tableware industry. William Leighton Sr., experimenting at Wheeling in 1864, developed a formula for producing high-quality colorless glass using soda lime in place of expensive and dangerous leads. Application of the formula meant that clear glass similar in weight and resonance to leaded glass could be produced less expensively, providing an ideal material for the mass production of patterned tableware. Since lime glass "set up" or became rigid more quickly than leaded glass, advances in the production process were needed so that glass could be worked more quickly. Changes in furnace design, fuel source, and the annealing of glass followed.

The same year that Leighton developed his soda lime formula, Pittsburgher Thomas Atterbury patented a continuous mechanical annealing

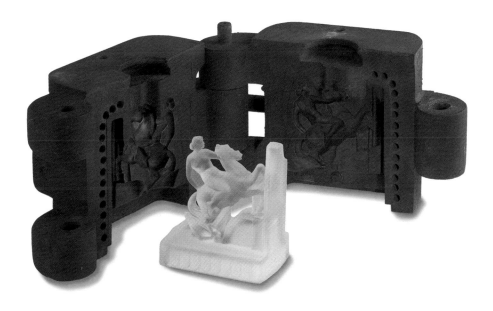

The metal mold used to press this glass bookend (c. 1940) from the Kenneth Haley Glass Co. in Greensburg weighs almost 100 pounds and took several hundred hours to create. Expensive to make, molds are rarely discarded.

furnace. Annealing was vital to glass production and quality control because as glass cools, the exterior cools most quickly, creating tension within the piece. Proper annealing, or slow cooling of the glass, resolves that tension and protects against brittleness, cracking, and breakage. Before 1865, annealing was done in kilns: glass was loaded in, the kiln was sealed, then heated, and later left to cool. Atterbury's mechanical "lehr," or oven, provided more control and management of the process, requiring less hand labor and production time. Atterbury's design was for a circular lehr, while innovations by others in Pittsburgh, such as Theodore Zeller, and elsewhere, led to the development of a linear lehr similar to that still in use today.

Furnace design and capacity were also crucial elements in achieving the full production potential of press mold technology. Pressing increased the speed of production, which demanded more melting capacity in the factory. In 1820, the average furnace pot held 700 pounds of melted batch — not sufficient to keep up with the needs of a press shop. Attempts were made to increase the size of the pots without decreasing the even melting of the batch, its ingredients, or the clarity of the glass. Philip Arbogast made an early attempt to develop a smokeless, cleaner-burning coal-fired furnace in 1873 when he patented the process of combining hot air with the coal gases just before they passed into the pot chamber.

Arbogast was one of a generation of Pittsburgh innovators who gained his experience on the factory floor working hot glass. With his brother Alexander,

Opposite page: The narrow neck of a flask (Pittsburgh's Lippincott, Fry & Co., 1866) prevented its manufacture by a press, so flasks continued to be blown well into the late 19th century. Below: Branding bottles (1870-1910) using "slug plates" — a bottle was blown in a mold with the plate inside, then the plate removed — allowed a company to brand the same bottle style for different clients.

he began his career as a glassblower in a South Side factory in the 1850s. The two were probably bottle blowers, for in 1860, Alexander began a bottle manufactory under the name Arbogast & Kapphahn. The partnership dissolved in 1861, though the business continued under Arbogast's management as a black bottle manufactory producing wine, brandy, porter, and schnapps bottles. Out of business by 1865, the brothers continued working as glassblowers, Philip working side-by-side with his sons J.L. and C.V. Arbogast.[12] In 1873, Philip Arbogast patented the process discussed above and assigned it to F.T. Plunkett and D.O. Cunningham, bottle manufacturers who were probably his employers. In 1881, he made a major technological contribution to the industry when he patented an early automated machine for blowing glass bottles.[13] The full application of automation would not be realized until the early 20th century, but Arbogast's machine signaled the future of glass production.

The discovery of rich sources of natural gas in the region and its application as a fuel brought changes to the factory floor and changes as well in the organization and location of factories. First used at the Rochester Tumbler Co. in Beaver County, natural gas became the industry's fuel of choice. It burned at a more constant and intense heat, was easier to control, and did not cause discoloration. There was much experimentation with introducing gas as a furnace fuel and with adapting furnace design to allow for the continuous production of glass. Movement was away from the smaller pot furnaces to larger tank furnaces, in which a new batch could be loaded at one end while molten glass was worked continuously at the other. By ensuring a steady supply of glass, workers were not idle while an individual pot heated to a usable state.

This fruit jar (c. 1867), patented by G.W. Buffington and made in Pittsburgh by Wm. Frank & Sons, was produced for only a few years and is the only jar of its type known to exist.

Many patents were filed from 1865 to 1885 on continuous tank production — some workable and some completely inapplicable. The Atterburys, schooled in the rich industrial milieu of Pittsburgh, borrowed from the reverberatory furnaces used in iron puddling for their furnace design.[14] John Vogel, an inventor living just north of Pittsburgh in Sharpsburg, simply replaced the interior of a pot furnace with a single tank.[15] One widely applied and copied design was devised by Charles Siemens, who patented a regenerative furnace in England (1875) and then in the United States (1880).[16] The Siemens continuous tank furnace was first used in the window glass industry. By combining continuous tank technology, the Wheeling soda lime formula of 1864, gas for fuel, and linear annealing lehrs, the full potential of pressing technology could be realized.

The annealing ovens may have been linear, but progress was not: technological innovation in the glass industry was a process of fits and starts, of forward and backward steps, of gains made and fortunes lost. Nor were innovations applied in all factories at once; in fact, hand manufacture continued to be used, and is in fact still used in Western Pennsylvania factories today. A balancing act occurred in the application of technology between finances, space, availability of fuels and raw materials, and acceptance by workers.

Change was a gradual and a not-always-agreeable or agreed-on process. What worked for one did not necessarily work for the many. Just as James O'Hara and Albert Gallatin struggled with the many facets of their businesses in the early 19th century, so too did the Cunninghams and the Atterburys and the glasshouse owners of the mid- to late 19th century battle to develop or buy or control the creative capital of their day.

Success, overall, was apparent. Between 1840 and 1885, factories in the southwestern corner of Pennsylvania increased from 26 to 61, as Pittsburgh became the heart of the nation's glass industry. Allegheny County boasted 51 of the country's 211 glassworks, while Beaver County had four, Fayette County three, and Lawrence County two, with one also under construction in Armstrong County. No county in the country came close to having the concentration of industry found in Allegheny, its nearest competition being Kings County, (Brooklyn) New York, home to 12 glassworks.[17]

Pittsburgh manufacturers, who for decades had benefited from their strategic location and access to raw materials, were, by the 1880s, reaping the rewards of the perpetual interplay of ideas and industry in the nation's most renowned "Machine Age town."

Not all benefited equally and not all would survive the changes that lay ahead in the late 19th century. What can be said, however, is that many of the elements that made large-scale production of pressed glass possible were in place, and, further, that major change brought about by the spread of automation also was afoot in the container and window glass industries. Expansion in Pittsburgh was constricted due to geography and other limitations that industrial enterprises faced in urban areas, so before the industry would reach its zenith in Western Pennsylvania, entrepreneurs in numerous other counties in the region — and new workers, many thousands of them below the age of 16 — would make their impact.

Made by F. & J. McKee of Pittsburgh from 1856 to 1860, these delicate fruit jars never "caught on" because of the difficulty of safely prying open their vacuum-sealed lids.

Part II

To increase production of glass required a reliable and constant supply of raw materials. Companies turning out a half-million pieces of glass a week, such as Rochester Tumbler, needed huge stores of raw materials, and those materials took up storage space at the factory; in addition, space was needed for mixing the materials, to prepare them for the furnaces. As late as 1880, glass factories still were largely concentrated in the densely populated, urban landscape of Pittsburgh's South Side, cheek-to-jowl with homes, businesses, churches, and schools, and landlocked between the Monongahela River and the sheer rock bluff of Mt. Washington towering over the valley. Little space existed for factories to expand. Rising city taxes and prohibitive laws regulating the dumping of by-products generated in the manufacturing process also contributed to the restrictiveness of Pittsburgh's South Side.[18]

It is during this period, as the interiors of factories were recast, that the distribution of the industry's manufacturing complexes also changed. Of paramount importance was the railroad: its spread freed the industry from reliance on the rivers. Likewise, the discovery of natural gas — first used as a fuel for industry in Western Pennsylvania during the 1870s — loosed the half-century-old tie to coal seams and forests. Anywhere the railroad ran and gas was available became a potential factory site.

Owners had long realized the possible applications of gas. Thomas Bakewell served on the gas lighting committee for the city of Pittsburgh in 1830s, and H. Sellers McKee served on a similar civic committee in the 1870s. A savvy businessman, McKee bought up farm land in outlying Westmoreland County described, in later accounts, as "3 1/2 miles west of Greensburg on the Pennsylvania Railroad and is the center of the grandest gas field in the state."[19] It is to this property, in 1888, that he moved his factory from Pittsburgh's South Side.

The Westmoreland County papers buzzed with news of McKee and James A. Chambers building "an exclusive city of glass in Pittsburgh's suburbs." In this new glass city, named "Jeannette" for McKee's wife, the Chambers window glass manufactory and McKee's tableware factory rose alongside dairy barns and farmhouses. With investment backing from a cadre of local industrialists as well as New York and Philadelphia "money men," McKee and Chambers built not only their factories but also a town, constructing houses and businesses and founding major institutions such as the bank. McKee's factory occupied a spacious 4.5 acres, while the Chambers-McKee window glass complex sprawled over 35 acres. Taking advantage of the chance to build from the ground up, both factories were fully integrated and applied the latest technology: transmission of batch from the mixing room to the furnace using a belt system; the continuous tank; air cooling systems for the factory floor, and the latest in other machinery. The new factories bore little resemblance to those left behind in Pittsburgh.[20]

The phenomenon was repeated throughout the region. Wherever natural gas surged below ground, factories rose above. By 1902, not only had the glass industry's growth again exploded, with 115 glassworks in 17 counties in the western half of Pennsylvania — Allegheny County 29, Westmoreland 14, Beaver 12, and Washington 9 — but one county, McKean, had 18 works where there had been none in 1885. The industry had also grown further west, blooming in the gas-rich states of Ohio (20 factories in 1885; 35 in 1902) and West Virginia (4 in 1885; 27 in 1902).[21]

In Western Pennsylvania, factory owners followed the lead of McKee and Chambers out of Pittsburgh and into the countryside, and new men entered the business. Glass became the main industry in new towns such as Jeannette

Opposite page: McKee Glass of Jeannette, Pa., commemorated the 50th anniversary of the town and its factory by issuing this plate in 1938.
Below: The impact of the Phoenix Glass Co. factory on its town, Monaca, Pa., is revealed in a 1920 photograph. The complex included rail spurs for bringing in raw materials and shipping out glass products.

and Ford City, and of vital importance to numerous other towns, such as Charleroi and Washington.

In Monaca, Beaver County, industrial plants included the Phoenix Glass Co., American Glass Specialty Co. and Opalite Tile Works, as well as Colonial Steel, the U.S. Sanitary Co., a brick works, the railroad, and a host of small concerns. Glass supplied about one-third of the town's workforce with skilled

Pittsburg, Pa., Blowing Bottles in Glass Factory.

Through the closing decades of the 19th century, boys were essential in the glasshouse operation — gathering glass, opening and closing the molds, and carrying glass to the annealing ovens.

and unskilled jobs. Even in 1908 and later, Phoenix was a big producer of blown ware, lamp shades, lighting devices, and vases; many of these products required skilled craftsman (blowers), while laborers, coopers, and teamsters rounded out the factory's force. On the other hand, American Glass Specialty primarily dealt in decorated ware, and most of its employees were women.[22] Cold processes, hand-painted decoration and acid-etching, and finishing, washing, and packing were often the purview of women workers. Rarely did a woman set foot in those areas of the factory where hot glass was worked and they always formed a small percentage of the total employees in the industry. In 1885, of 6,053 glassworkers in Allegheny County, only 141 were women.[23]

Boys under the age of 16, however, were of crucial importance. Among those 6,053 glassworkers in 1885, 1,470 were "children and youths" under 16.[24] Boys had always been a part of the glasshouse workforce. Elbridge Gerry, visiting Pittsburgh in 1813, recorded in his diary: "Small boys with facility, completely formed a cruet, in the glasshouse in less time than 30 seconds."[25] James Bryce, introduced in Chapter 2, documented his entry into factory life in the 1820s at age 11; his journals provide a startling glimpse at conditions for child laborers. As the industry grew, so, too, did the core group of children, such as the mold boys in the bottle factories, crouching at the feet of their masters, opening and closing the blow molds hundreds of times a day. Others were gatherers and "carrying boys," "tending boys" and packers, "sticker-ups" and cleaning boys. They did the lifting and the placing and the sweeping — the dozens of tasks small and large that no glasshouse owner wanted to pay a man's wages for. In young James Bryce's day, they brought home $1.25 a week, while in 1885 their pay ranged from 30 cents to $1 a day.[26]

Their work was hot and dirty, the tasks repetitive and dulling. Glasshouses that ran 24 hours a day required boys to work all shifts, through the day and all night. After work, they went to homes such as those in Sharpsburg's "Glass House Row" on Main Street, described by Elizabeth Beardsley Butler in 1914:

Each of its eight houses was divided into two dwellings of two rooms each, and the tenants who lived in the front house had to pass through their neighbors living room or walk around the square to reach the vault (outhouse) in the rear. There were four vaults (one overfilled and out of use) and but two outside hydrants for the 18 families in this row. Waste water was thrown into the street sewers. The basements of the houses were of little use as they were flooded when the river was high.[27]

Organizations founded to eliminate child labor pointed to the region's glasshouses as examples of the system's horrors. A full-page advertisement in the *Saturday Evening Post*, placed by the National Child Labor Committee, began, "If you could look for a moment into the great glass factories of New Jersey or western Pennsylvania... and see the pinched faces and the shriveled forms of little children who are doomed to spend their childhood years at work... your heart would go out to these children and your purse would be opened to the people who are trying to pass laws to rescue these little ones from disease and premature old age."[28]

Glass companies vigorously fought the child labor laws, often winning exemption from regulation. For instance, with the introduction of the continuous tank, most glasshouses worked three shifts. When regulations were passed to prohibit night work for children under 16 years of age, the glass industry fought the provision and was exempted. By 1908, two-thirds of boys employed in Pennsylvania glass factories were working nights. Often bonuses were offered to encourage night work, but some factories made it a condition

Macbeth-Evans' illustrious Dogwood pattern (c. 1925) was among the first tableware lines made using automation.

Opposite page: Thomas Evans (c. 1910) was a founder of Macbeth-Evans, a Pittsburgh glassmaker which, to avoid being swamped by low-cost automated producers, invested early and heavily in technology. At its peak, Macbeth-Evans made over 20 million lamp chimneys a year. One style had a painted house with blank windows where the light shone through. Above: Note the differences in shape between the Macbeth-Evans chimneys, left, and the model, right, patented by Pittsburgher Edward Dithridge in 1861 that was said to be cleaner-burning.

of employment.[29] Boys also were subject to the same rotation in shifts as adult workers, working a week of days then a week of nights.

Glasshouse owners clearly recognized the value of this cheap labor. A letter sent by the Central Glass Works of Wheeling to 43 glass companies in Pennsylvania, West Virginia, Ohio, and Indiana calls on glass companies to organize against a child labor reform law being considered in the U.S. Congress (the date of the letter is not known): "[W]e really believe this Bill would never have been reported out of the Judiciary Committee, had those vitally interested, shown the proper spirit, and counteracted the Propaganda in favor of it."[30] The letter closes by making clear the interests of glass manufacturers: "A little money spent by each factory, would be nothing to compare with the Glass Factories' being compelled to hire men to do boys' work."[31]

Child labor increasingly became an issue of national concern. Glass factory owners, who battled to corral the reform movement in the state legislatures, in hopes of heading off federal action, lost to the journalists, documentary photographers, and social activists who took the issue directly to a national audience. Ironically, as the attention of Congress and the public focused on restrictive laws, machines were being conceived to replace the jobs held by children.

The child labor issue had a special resonance for the bottle and container industry. In 1880, nearly one-third of the youths in the glass industry nationwide worked in green glass (container) factories.[32] Just one year after that count was made, however, Pittsburgher Philip Arbogast introduced a semi-automated bottle-blowing machine. His invention worked particularly well on

As reform laws began to restrict child labor in the early 20th century, automation, such as bottle-blowing machines, made much of their work obsolete. Michael Owens' invention lowered labor costs on a gross of beer bottles, for example, from $1.47 to a dime. Opposite page: Heisey Glass Co. produced busts in 1927 of Michael Owens as gifts to customers and friends of the Owens Bottle Machine Co.

wide-mouth jars, such as fruit jars, and was put into operation in non-union shops in Huntington, West Virginia, and in Beaver Falls. The American Flint Glass Workers Union recognized the technology would replace skilled blowers, and prevented its use by Daniel Ripley of Pittsburgh, and in other union shops. Other companies, Atlas Glass Co. (later Hazel Atlas Glass Co.) of Washington, Pennsylvania, and Greensburg Glass Co. among them, began experimenting to improve the Arbogast design or to develop similar machines.[33]

Arbogast's work had built on earlier experiments by Michael Owens and his team of engineers and machinists at Libbey Glass in Toledo. Years later, in 1894, Owens and his team would develop a paste mold machine for mechanically blowing light bulbs. That breakthrough drove companies such as Phoenix Glass Co. of Monaca, where bulbs were hand-blown, out of the light bulb business. By 1895, Owens had adapted the machinery to the automated production of lamp chimneys and tumblers.[34]

Pittsburgh firms, such as those run by Thomas Evans and George Macbeth — world leaders in the hand-production of lamp chimneys — realized that without control of the Owens machine, their companies would fold. In 1899, Evans' and Macbeth's companies joined to bid for the exclusive right to use Owens' patented machines. A handwritten account by Thomas Evans documents the negotiations. The chief bidder against Evans and Macbeth was the flint glass union. Founded in Pittsburgh in 1878, this powerful union was fully aware of the implications of automated technology. Michael Owens had cause to consider the union's bid. Having risen from the factory floor, Owens had been intimately involved in the politics of the union, and became a powerful leader in Local 9 out of Wheeling. But he also realized, as did his financier Edward Drummond Libbey, that the future of the glass industry lay with machinery, not skilled men. Still, purchasing the Owens machinery cost Macbeth and Evans dearly: each put up $250,000 in cash for the rights and an additional $50,000 to purchase a Toledo factory operated by Libbey-Owens.

Macbeth and Evans were also careful to maintain their relationships with the men from Toledo. Libbey served as an officer in the newly formed company and as an investor in later ventures. He also encouraged the Pittsburgh company to continue to invest in the innovations coming out of his Ohio R&D center. In 1909, Macbeth-Evans purchased an automated bottle-blowing machine from the Owens Bottle Machine Co. in Toledo.[35] The inventiveness of Michael Owens, with the venture capital of Thomas Evans, George Macbeth, and Edward Libbey, proved itself on several occasions to be a powerful and lucrative consortium.

The semi-automatic bottle machines borrowed key design features from

For location of towns and factories in this chapter, see maps on page 158.

pressed glass machines such as the rotary tables designed by Washington Beck and others. (Such equipment enabled one press machine to work multiple molds by rotating them to the plunger, speeding up the pressing process.) With Owens' innovations, a paste mold semi-automatic machine with a three-man crew could produce 4,300 jars a day, a 15 percent increase over hand-production. The machine crew was also cheaper, as it could be formed of unskilled laborers rather than the more expensive skilled union hands.[36]

In 1903, Owens introduced the first automatic machine that produced narrow-mouth vessels, such as beer and soda bottles. Libbey and Owens established their new company (Owens Bottle Machine Co.) to build and license the machines. Unlike the semi-automatics, this machine gathered the glass, as well as mechanically blowing and forming the bottles. Once a belt was added to move the bottles to the lehr, the machine could be run by just a mechanic who monitored and serviced the equipment. In 1906, the company reported that the Owens machine reduced labor costs on a gross of beer bottles to 10 cents, compared to 75 cents if made by semi-automatic machine and $1.47 if made by hand. Within seven years of introduction, 100 Owens machines were producing 360 million bottles a year.[37]

John Lubbers invented machines that drew huge cylinders of glass up to 40 feet tall, rendering skilled blowers of window glass obsolete.

As a result, child laborers in the glass industry dropped nationally by almost half, from 6,435 to 3,561, with the manual work more and more done by conveyor belts and various other mechanical devices. Legislation did its part in removing children from the glasshouse, but so, too, did technology.[38]

In the container industry, meanwhile, machines were introduced relatively slowly, both to prevent prices from plummeting and also to avoid inflaming the union. Owens Bottle licensed its machinery only to manufacturers already in business. It took a full 20 years for the industry to become automated, balancing increased demand with job losses. As late as 1924-25, national output stood at 25.9 billion bottles produced by 1,000 skilled blowers, 300 semi-automatic machines, and 1,500 operators using automatic machines. The automatic machine, while eliminating skilled work in one part of the factory, created demand for 1,500 new mechanics by 1925.[39]

As might be expected, the Pittsburgh region remained near the forefront nationally in container manufacturing. In 1880, even before Philip Arbogast's machine technology was deployed, New Jersey was first but Pennsylvania ranked second in output among all states. Bottles, one of the earliest items made in the western region of Pennsylvania, were a mainstay throughout the hand-production period of the 19th century, and also after the widespread application of machine operations in the early 20th century. Well-known concerns during this period included Cunningham Co. on Pittsburgh's South Side, J.T.A. Hamilton in the Strip District, and Thomas Wightman, with factories in Pittsburgh and around the region.

A similar process of gradually introducing automatic machinery also occurred in the manufacture of flat glass — first allowing less expense and higher quality for making small pieces, such as window panes; eventually, however, technologies devised for making large plate glass pieces, such as department store windows, were applied to all flat glass production. Change was rapid after about 1885, the year that Pittsburgh furnace- and pot-builder Thomas Nicholson commented, "There has been no substantial progress made in the structure of window glass furnaces, no indeed in the window glass business, in the last fifty years."[40] An exception was the "swing pit," which allowed workers to stand above deep pits and swing the blown cylinders as gravity elongated and englarged the forms. In addition, the continuous tank, and advances in both melting and annealing furnaces, provided a steady supply of high-quality glass; otherwise, however, Nicholson was right: production methods had changed little.

It took the work of John Lubbers at the research and development facility built for him by James Chambers at the American Window Glass Co. to revo-

Although flat glass became a high-tech business, this image from the Pittsburgh Plate Glass plant in Creighton, Pa. (c. 1910), shows the laborers needed to inspect, pack, and ship the glass.

lutionize the trade. Lubbers, a window glass flattener, experimented for almost 10 years with the design of his machine to replicate the blowing process of a skilled worker. The system involved a circular "bait," attached to a source of compressed air and suspended over a pot containing enough molten batch to produce a single cylinder up to 40 feet in length. As the bait was raised, drawing the glass cylinder with it, air was pumped into the cylinder to prevent it from collapsing. When the pot was empty and the cylinder had cooled slightly, it was lowered onto a series of supports. The ends of the cylinder were removed, the cylinder was scored, and it was then transported to the ovens, where it was flattened and annealed. Panes were cut from these large sheets of glass, then packed and shipped to market.

The Lubbers process replicated hand technology — flat glass still started its life as a cylinder — but the intricate ballet of hand production, of skilled blowers manipulating 8-foot-long glass balloons, was gone. Some displaced blowers and gatherers, many of them Belgian immigrants, found work in the remaining hand factories, but many more found no slots at all, their places filled by unskilled workers most often of Italian and Eastern European ancestry. American Window Glass introduced the Lubbers machine slowly to factories in its consortium to temper reaction from the union, even though that machine merely presaged an even more revolutionary wave: the drawing of glass from a machine in a flat, rather than circular, form.

Three processes — the Colburn, Fourcault, and Pittsburgh Plate processes — differed in how the sheet was started (whether formed or annealed) but were all drawn continuously from a tank. The Colburn machines were developed by Irving Colburn. In 1912, Michael Owens convinced Edward Libbey to invest in the process and to purchase the patent rights; four years later, Libbey-Owens Sheet Glass Co. incorporated, and by 1920, the firm was selling sheet-drawing machines around the world.[41] (The Colburn machines were first used in a Charleston, West Virginia, plant in 1917.) The Fourcault process was developed in Belgium and Czechoslovakia after World War I and was introduced in the United States in 1923, while Pittsburgh Plate Glass Co. developed a similar process at about the same time.

Pennsylvania had been the nation's unrivaled leader in window glass production for many decades, producing 44 percent of America's output in 1880 (almost four times as much as the nearest rival, New York),[42] with glassworks on the western edge of the Keystone State dominating the flat glass trade, using cylinder technology. That technology had improved the quality of flat glass — whatever imperfections remained were not objectionable in small sheets and panes — but innovations in the manufacture of distortion-free glass in very large pieces was still to come.

Very little plate glass was produced in America until the late 1800s. (There were only five plate glass works in the entire country.) Most plate glass was expensively cast, ground, and polished, and imported from France, England, and Belgium. Raw materials were melted in regenerative pot furnaces, and the individual pots were removed from the furnace by crane, skimmed, and then emptied onto large iron tables. As the molten glass was poured, a large cast iron roller passed over it, producing a coarse flat sheet. After being annealed, then allowed to cool, the sheet was finished to the desired thickness on circular tables using an elaborate system of grinding machinery, sand, emery, and water; final polishing occurred using felt. During the last two decades of the 19th century, however, new players such as the American Window Glass Co. and Pittsburgh Plate Glass Co. (1883) entered the flat glass marketplace and the resulting changes were rapid and wide-reaching.

PPG's innovations in the 1920s opened a still newer chapter in the Pittsburgh region's eminence in flat glass — most notably, at PPG's Ford City and Creighton factories. The company's semi-continuous ribbon process for plate glass was first tried in 1922, while innovations after 1924 fully automated the creation of the plate-glass "blank" and the grinding and polishing operations. In 1928, PPG's "Pittsburgh Process," which vertically drew a continuous sheet of molten glass in a four-story-tall forming and cooling line, minimized imperfections and increased speed for making window glass. Glass made in this way was marketed as "PENNVERNON Glass." Continuous processes produced finished products from raw materials in just 10 hours. They also allowed incredible control over the thickness and quality of the

By 1920, the scale of glass factories was immense: workers draw huge ladles of molten glass from furnaces at PPG's Creighton factory.

Testing Room, Consolidated Lamp & Glass Co., Coraopolis, Pa.

glass, and saved production time: to blow 50 square feet of glass took a man almost five hours, while sheet-drawn glass took only one-half of 1 "machine man-hour."[43]

Continuous, automated production of plate glass was not instituted in the United States, however, until 1963, when PPG applied the British Pilkington Process. This patented process for "float glass" produced a ribbon of molten glass floating in a bath of molten tin. Produced in huge horizontal furnaces and linked to continuous lehrs, the thickness of the glass is controlled by moving the blank through a series of rollers as it cools and hardens. The glass is cut to the desired size while on the line, and then stacked and packed by machine or hand, depending on the factory. Quality control occurs directly in the line: flawed glass pieces are dumped into a chute, transported by conveyor back to the mixing room, and remixed. Human hands direct the computers which run the machinery, while ceramic and glass engineers monitor the line, but glass can be produced from start to finish and never touched by man.

In the other important sector of the industry, glass tableware, the technology for its automated production was in place by the 1920s. Macbeth-Evans, which had purchased the first developed automated process for lamp chimneys in 1899, put its engineers to work on applying that technology for tableware. Mechanical engineer Charles Schuck experimented with the development of molds that would coordinate with the automated machines, and by 1930, the tableware lines were fully automated. Macbeth-Evans advertisements celebrated the new technology with call lines such as "A Quality Shape … for Quantity Sales," or "Styled for quality… priced for volume."[44]

Other companies in the Pittsburgh region also adapted automation. A 1928 *China, Glass & Lamps* article describes the automated lines at Jeannette Glass Co., where machines controlled the process from production of the ware to finishing and polishing:

> [F]irst of all it was necessary to build two especially designed continuous tanks. With these tanks, new mould cooling and block cooling equipment also had to be furnished. It was also necessary to design new parts for the automatic machines and devise new methods for polishing the ware made, for it is in the polishing of colored ware that the brilliant lustre and life is obtained. In order to do this, several especially built glazing and polishing machines were purchased from A.B. Knight of Fairmount, W. Va., and one was erected in the factory by the company's engineers who are experimenting at all time on

Glass firms employed women almost exclusively in finishing departments (inset, Consolidated Lamp & Glass, c. 1910) as decorators, inspectors, cleaners, and packers, and as office workers. The evocative image of Mary Bell Thomas, center, and her colleagues was taken in 1917 at U.S. Glass on Pittsburgh's South Side.

improved methods of manufacturing. From the finishing machines the ware is carried to automatic lehrs where it is properly annealed.[45]

This new machinery allowed the company to turn out 50 tons of glass daily. Though all of the work at Jeannette Glass was automated, this is not to say that automation replaced hand or pressing techniques throughout the industry. In fact, both techniques are still in use today, especially in the table glass industry.

Even in hand production, however, new technology made inroads, especially in replacing repetitive or dangerous tasks in the factory. A company such as Lenox, in Mt. Pleasant, Pennsylvania, which specializes in handmade table glass, now uses belt systems to carry finished pieces to the lehrs for annealing. Bottle-makers such as Glenshaw Glass Co., headquartered in the Pittsburgh suburb of Glenshaw, use pneumatic lifts to move glass once moved by manual labor. American Video Glass, opened just in 1997, is not only fully automated, but makes extensive use of robots to lift, move, and support the 50- to 75- pound pieces of glass produced for use in television sets. While automated machines do provide a savings in labor costs for the company, they also make the workplace safer. The most recent innovations in automation — computer-driven systems and robotics — also require better-educated or better-trained workers, forcing further changes on the factory floor.

In considering the full sweep of technological change in the glass industry, we see that until 1830, evolution proceeded at a snail's pace. Some 2,000 years separated the two major advances in production — the introduction of the blowpipe and then of mechanical pressing in 1830. Thereafter, however, change proceeded at a dizzying pace. Innovations, whether developed in the advanced machine culture of Pittsburgh or elsewhere in the nation, were quickly adopted or adapted throughout the industry. The industry in Western Pennsylvania, which had faced a mighty struggle in its first few decades, came into its own in the mid-19th century. Blessed with plentiful natural resources, a growing cadre of skilled workers, and access to both the intellectual and financial capital of an industrializing metropolis, glassmaking flourished in the lands along Western Pennsylvania's three rivers.

Local industrialists financed the development and application of the machine technology that reordered the factory system. Within a century of the hand press' appearance, the industry bore little resemblance to the small shops of Gallatin and O'Hara. Every stage of production had changed, from the preparation and processing of the "batch," to furnace design, to the machinery needed for making and annealing glass. In size, layout, and location, the glass factory was wholly modern. Processes never imagined to be done by any force other than human were accomplished routinely without man's touch. The hands of the skilled craftsman were replaced first by the levered arms of presses and then by robotic arms. The craftsman's breath was re-created by mechanical lungs, his mind by computers and automated networks.

As the 20th century advanced, companies that invested in technology and in research into more technology were the ones that prospered. Machine and chemical technology not only transformed production in the glass industry but also made its mass-produced objects available for vast new markets and an entirely new breed of individual consumer.

Pressing, the chief innovation in a century of technological wonders in glassmaking, created a plethora of choices. Inexpensive chemicals made colorless glass, once a luxury because of the cost of the lead needed to make it, affordable for mass audiences. Note the range of shapes and colors using only one pattern — Adams and Co.'s "Wildflower" (1875-1900).

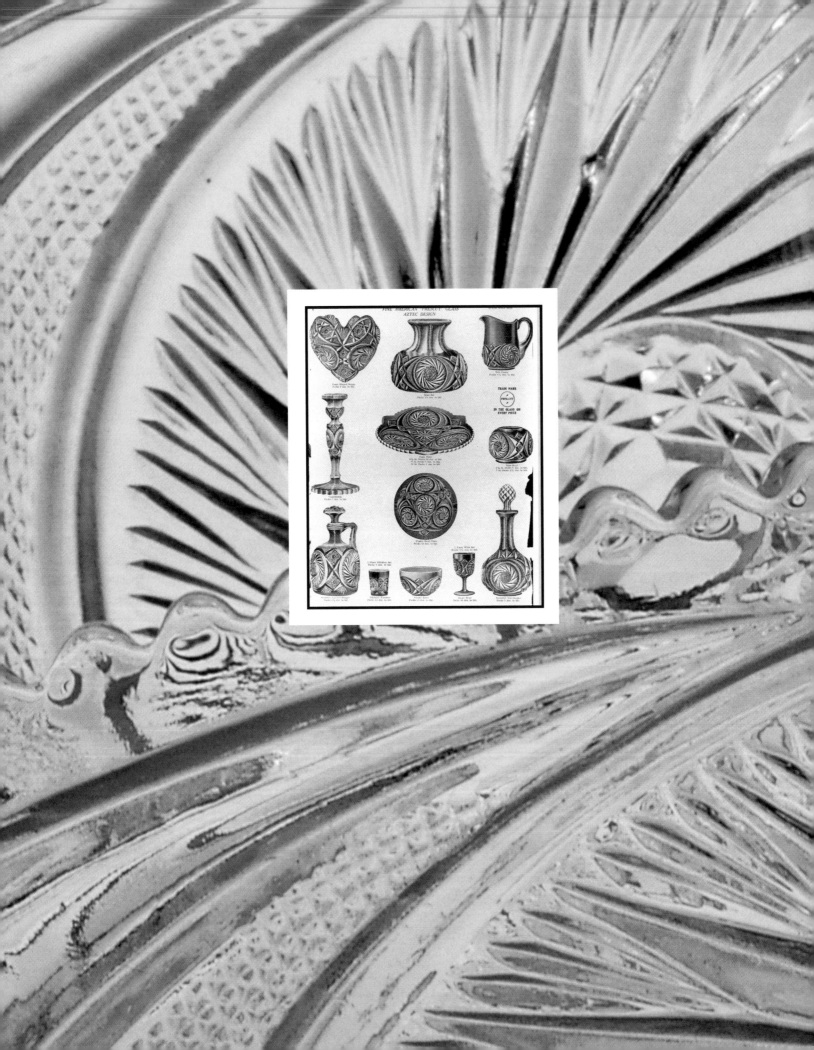

SHATTERING
NOTIONS

CHAPTER 4

Selling

In addition to learning how to make glass, companies wrestled with creating and meeting demand for their products. Marketing strategies included the use of catalogs (opposite page, McKee Glass, c. 1915), and devising new products for fresh markets. McKee's punch bowl (c. 1910), for example, traded on the age-old luxury appeal of cut glass, though it was made less expensively from colorless pressed glass.

Often overlooked in the history of glass is the fact that glasshouse owners spent as much time during the industry's early years attending to the marketing and selling of glass as they did to producing it. In 1797, when production in the region commenced, Western Pennsylvania sat on the edge of the frontier, and, unlike their eastern competitors, glassmakers on the frontier did not have established markets or systems for sales and distribution. Growth in production required staking out a commercial presence and selling wares in parts of the country where few American firms had previously tried. To understand the industry's advances, it is essential to examine how men such as James O'Hara handled the selling of his products.

Decades after O'Hara, in the years right after the Civil War when Western

Pennsylvania became the production capital of the nation, the need to market and sell was similarly magnified. As we shall see, to lead in production meant little for Pittsburgh in a highly competitive economy without also being the leading marketplace city for glass. Techniques commonly associated today with the selling and marketing of consumer goods, such as annual trade shows, were introduced to America's glass industry in Pittsburgh, by Pittsburghers. Once established, the city's glassmakers built their reputations decade after decade; for well over half a century, Pittsburgh and the firms that spread out from the city's crowded downtown in the late 1800s formed the merchandising core. Just as their predecessors had excelled at marketing and production alike, glassmakers during the city's industrialization era proved as capable in the fine art of sales as they were at inventing and applying the new machine technologies of the period.

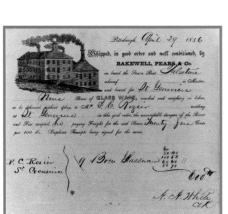

Billheads such as this one for Bakewell, Pears & Co. from 1846, provide insights about company and customer alike.

To track the evolution of selling glass, one must start with the glass business in Western Pennsylvania in the period of its founding, when, like most enterprises of the era, commerce was extraordinarily personal. Merchant-manufacturers such as James O'Hara, whose foray into glass was examined thoroughly in Chapter 2, called on contacts in business that he had nurtured over many years to yield not only improvements in the speed and quality of production, but also to help him market and sell his products.

O'Hara's former quartermaster position in the military, as well as his extensive holdings in real estate on the western frontier, introduced him to many others with entrepreneurial interests. Time and again, partners in non-glass ventures — for instance, James Morrisson of Lexington, Kentucky, an investor with O'Hara in real estate — helped him merchandise and distribute glassware to the west and south of Pittsburgh. Morrisson went so far as to consider starting his own factory, but O'Hara's counsel about his firm's difficulties appears to have dissuaded Morrisson.[1]

The nature of commerce during the period of O'Hara's prominence made it natural that family members, trusted friends, and business partners were relied on to a large extent to help with the selling of glass. Accounting procedures and the constant shortage of specie meant that much business was conducted on faith and credit. O'Hara's payment terms were usually defined as credit for a period up to six months or a commission of 5 percent over Pittsburgh prices.[2] He often sought opportunities to integrate his business ventures so that they might profit from one another. His hollowware business, for example, supplied porter bottles for his brewery, enlarging the territory for his beer well beyond the much shorter range that beer casks could be transported.

His ship-building business also gave him occasion to transport glass down the Ohio River at reduced cost. In 1805, his son William was charged with overseeing the voyage of O'Hara's new ship, the *General Butler*, from Pittsburgh to New Orleans and then on to Liverpool, England. The ship set sail from Pittsburgh stocked with local products, including O'Hara's glass and porter. William was instructed to sell both items in Louisville, with any remainders to be taken down the Ohio River to the Mississippi River, and on to Natchez, a thriving southern port. In addition, O'Hara advised his son, "You may think it proper to take a few boxes and barrels to New Orleans, to try that market, which may be a good experiment."[3] O'Hara goes on to make clear his reasons for trying such markets:

Early utilitarian objects such as bottles — these, primarily for storing household liquids, came from Fayette County companies (c. 1825) — were very similar in color and design, in a highly competetive marketplace. Being able to secure customers across an extensive area allowed one glassmaker to prosper at the expense of others.

> As my particular object in forwarding these few specimens of my own manufacturing to those places is in order to ascertain how far I may calculate on their custom in future; you will be very particular at each respecting probable demand or consumption, & forward such orders as you may procure for any quantity of glass or porter that may be required, which shall be duly executed.[4]

Clearly, O'Hara intends his son to develop new customers, as well as to calculate demand.

Not all glass, however, found its way west in boxes and barrels shipped by manufacturers; a lot of it made the journey in luggage and packs of individual travellers. And much of that sales activity occurred in the bustling commercial bazaar along Pittsburgh's Monongahela Wharf, where Eastern U.S. and international distibutors, and Pittsburgh firms, stored and staged shipments of every conceivable sort bound for the young nation's interior. By 1815, most Pittsburgh glasshouses had both a factory site and a downtown warehouse where goods were displayed and sold at retail. O'Hara, in 1811, built his three-story brick warehouse at the Point and kept it stocked with window glass, hollowware, and other products from his factory.[5] The tens of thousands of people who passed through Pittsburgh each year shopped from warehouse to warehouse, provisioning themselves for new lives on the frontier. Travellers' accounts describe the atmosphere along the wharf as

> one of the most animated scenes we have witnessed in a long time. Twenty steamboats lie at the landing taking in cargo for Louisville, St. Louis, Nashville, New Orleans.... The whole of our broad levee, from the bridge to Ferry Street, is closely dotted with drays and wagons, hurrying to the margin of the river from every point of access.... The margin of the wharf is absolutely covered to the height of a man with freight in all its varieties... the fronts of the great forwarding houses

are blocked by piles of boxes, bales and barrels in beautiful disorder. Shippers, porters, draymen and steamboat clerks blend their hurried voices at once — one is actually deafened with their cheerful din and rush of business.[6]

Period paintings show two- and three-story warehouse buildings along the waterfront, and an illustration from an 1850 ad in the Pittsburgh city directory provides a good frontal view of the Curling, Robertson & Co. warehouse. In addition, some Pittsburgh companies, such as Bakewell, which built a warehouse in Wheeling in the 1830s, extended their influence in the marketplace and enhanced their profits by opening branches in other cities.[7]

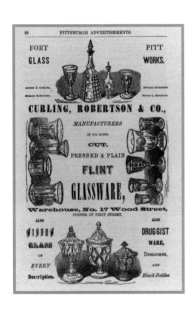

While glass during this period could be bought in Pittsburgh directly from the manufacturer's warehouse or from local commission and forwarding merchants, it also could be purchased routinely at auctions. The expense books of Pittsburgh banker John Thaw document that he bought the bulk of his glassware for home use at auctions. However, on one occasion in 1818, he does visit the Bakewell warehouse and notates his purchase as "cash pd. Bakewell & Co. for Lamp $15 Saltcellars 6. — Decanter 2$ — $23."[8]

Newspapers, the primary source of public information during the period, were also vital to the growth of the region's glass industry: they carried the first printed advertising. Advertisements in the *Pittsburgh Gazette* usually listed items produced by a glasshouse, and sometimes included prices. By the 1820s, newspaper ads were often illustrated with simple sketches. An announcement of new business partnerships or billheads might also carry an illustration, though the factory, and not its products, was usually depicted. Other opportunities for print advertising during these busy years of migration and settlement by European Americans were maps; for instance, Patrick Mulvaney listed both his cabinetry shop and his glass factory on an 1830 map of Pittsburgh.

Newspaper stories and travel accounts helped as well to establish the reputation of the region's products. Certain companies, especially the Bakewell company, also used presentation objects made for the French general Lafayette or U.S. presidents, as a means of associating their name with quality, for an exclusive clientele. Reports in the press about Bakewell's engraving and cutting, or about an award the firm received from the Franklin Institute, or concerning the company's new products, such as sulphide tumblers, further enhanced that reputation. In fact, by the 1830s, Pittsburgh glass had a reputation as quality merchandise. Retailers such as George Worthington of Cleveland specifically listed himself as an agent for Pittsburgh glass, while the Galena, Illinois, newspaper of February 20, 1836, announced, "GLASSWARE. Just received per steamboat Dubuque direct from Pittsburg, 24 boxes, containing Tumblers, Wines, Pitchers, Creams and Decanters, all for sale low by June 10."⁹ The inclusion of "Pittsburgh" in such descriptions — rather than a generic reference — attests to the mark of quality associated at an early date with the city's glassware.

The introduction of lithography to Pittsburgh changed how the region's glass products were presented both to retailers and to the buying public. In 1849, two men battled to complete the first lithographed representation of the city. Lithographed imagery shortly became desirable and popular, and its production methods were by the mid-1850s applied to illustrating and advertising the region's products. In 1856, the first advertisement appeared in a Pittsburgh city directory that illustrated the product line of a local glass manufacturer. The ad, for the Fort Pitt Works of Curling, Robertson & Co., shows 16 pieces of glass tableware framing a central description of the factory, providing its warehouse location, and listing its wares. Notable as an advertising piece, it also serves historians and collectors today as a way of documenting the company's pieces.

Illustrated trade catalogs and printed price lists suitable as broadsides also began appearing in the middle years of the century. O'Hara mentions catalogs and printed price lists in his correspondence; a price list exists from 1837 for the Wheeling factory of Francis Plunkett and Co.; and a price list for bottles from 1846 exists in the Historical Society of Western Pennsylvania Archives. This particular document is notable, for it reads at the top, "List of Prices... Adopted by the Western Glass Blowers, assembled in Mass Convention in Pittsburgh, June 22, 1846." The list illustrates the desire by either container manufacturers or bottle blowers (it is unclear which) to both develop and organize the marketplace through the establishment of set prices or set work rates.

The first known illustrated trade catalogs for Western Pennsylvania glass date from the late 1850s and early 1860s, and were designed for a variety of uses. They could be sent by manufacturers to their established merchandisers, so those retailers could both gather and place orders. They could also be carried by the growing force of travelling agents and salesmen. A few companies had used travelling agents all along. O'Hara's son, William, sometimes acted in that capacity during the early decades of the century — working down-river, developing new business and taking orders, while also collecting debts

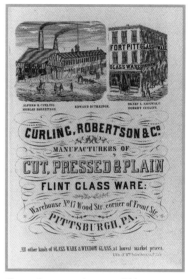

Opposite page, bottom: This unusual pressed sugar bowl, c. 1855, is believed to be an "advertising piece" for a company in the Pittsburgh region. Note the designs of objects on each panel of the bowl — apparently intended to showcase the company's merchandise. Above and opposite page, top: Curling, Robertson & Co. was a downtown Pittsburgh glassmaker. As lithographed images became typical in advertising during the 1850s, glassmakers could display pictures of their wares. Glass objects are on display in the warehouse windows on the far right in the image above.

from established clients.

Pittsburgher Tom Pears acted in that capacity for the Bakewell company from 1820 to 1822. Pears had a long relationship with the Bakewells and was related to them by marriage. He began working for the family in 1814 by establishing a sawmill in Henderson, Kentucky. Two years later, he began travelling on glass business for the Bakewells, even journeying to England

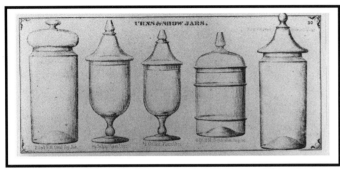

and France to recruit workers. Carrying a letter of introduction from Bakewell's glass cutter, whose last name was "Jardelle," Pears traveled throughout France searching for skilled cutters and trying to buy the designs for a French glass furnace. Carrying too little cash to entice workers to emigrate, he returned to New York with no glassblowers and only one cutter in tow. He was more successful on his second trip, which lasted two months in 1818, returning with "4 Blowers, 4 Garcon, 2 Gammains and a director."[10]

The Bakewell glass company sold many of the everyday items in its line for several decades. Among the objects that company sales agent Tom Pears sold throughout the Ohio River Valley in the 1820s were jars (though these date from about 1875).

Tom Pears briefly tried his hand at management, opening a black bottle manufactory near the Bakewell works in 1819. The factory failed, in the bargain wiping out his wife Sarah's inheritance, and Tom Pears once again went to work for his relatives. In January of 1820, he began exclusively plying inland waterways, selling glass and collecting debts owed to the Bakewells. Letters between Tom and Sarah Pears from this period allow us inside the business of marketing and distributing Pittsburgh glass in a particularly personal way.

Pears' work took him down the Ohio River to Pittsburgh's southern neighbor, Cincinnati, and Nashville. He not only arranged and managed the shipment of glass from town to town, primarily by steamboat but sometimes by keelboat, but he also traveled overland between river towns selling glass in the countryside. So elemental was river trade to the building of economic networks that Pears expresses gratitude for a snowstorm that stalls the steamboats behind his own sales mission. "I am glad of it," he writes, "for I have been able to sell scarcely anything here; but as glass is not very plentiful, if they [the other boats] do not arrive, I hope to sell most of what is here shortly."[11]

Pears also appears to have run auctions of glass in some of the towns he visits. In Nashville in 1820, he reports, "I am still here and doing very little — raffling, from which I hope and believe to have sold a good deal of the fine glass.... I shall leave here in a day or two and return in five or six days, and if in that time I cannot raffle anything away, shall leave the glass and start homeward."[12] What Pears did not "raffle" at auction, he left to be sold by Nashville merchants on credit. Of course, Pears then revisited the merchants to collect payment for whatever sold. (The collected money was sometimes enclosed in letters to Sarah, for her to transfer to the company.)

A further example of the personal nature of selling Pittsburgh glass in the industry's early days is that Pears mentions on occasion that Mr. Bakewell is with him, helping unpack and display the glass for the next day's sale. At other times, Bakewell and Pears worked different parts of the same territory simultaneously, their paths periodically crossing. In May of 1820, Pears writes to his wife, he and Bakewell connected in Cincinnati:

When I first saw your uncle the arrangement he proposed, and which I thought the best that could be adopted, was that he should go to Nashville by land, collecting what he could by the way, whilst I proceeded by water to the same place collecting and selling all I could on the road. From thence I was to go to St. Louis and collect what I could on my return. Since I have been here however he seems to wish to return home; and whether I go from here to the Falls [near Louisville] by water or land depends on getting a boat to take the glass from here to Nashville.... Mr. Bakewell, I believe I may say, seems pleased that I am here. He believes I may do something in the selling line at Nashville and he has not been there. But as I told you before leaving, it's quite useless travelling over the ground where he has been. The glass which he sold last fall and this spring is yet undisposed of, and money is so scarce people will not buy more.[13]

Pears makes scant reference to the type of glass he is selling. He does

While recruiting glassblowers in England, William Price convinced two potters (named Vodrey and Frost) to come to Pittsburgh. After establishing a ceramics company in the city, the duo thanked him with a personalized decorated pitcher that included a depiction of Price's employer. A valuable pitcher, it is the region's oldest known example of yellow ware (1828).

complain in June of 1820 that he has "too many goods of one kind for such an undertaking, and in leaving Pittsburgh… could not get such things as were wanted." A month later, he talks about selling the "fine glass," meaning, most likely, lead or "flint" glass tableware. He despairs of selling any glass at all in many areas where sophistication rivaled cash as the chief scarcity; in western Kentucky, he complains, "I believe there is not $50 of glass in the place, and they are never likely for the town to want much; for it is like Smithland a miserable hole. But if they wanted ever so much they have not the money to buy."[14]

Opposite page: By the 1850s, glassmakers had resolved technical problems with molds and had moved from "lacy" patterns to geometric designs similar to cut glass. The ovals on this Bakewell "Argus" compote (c. 1860) relect and refract light and shadow.

Pears worked between and on the rivers during years that the nation's economy was still burdened by fallout from the War of 1812 — severe economic depression persisted in many parts of the West well into the 1820s — and many merchants must have dreaded the sight of him. He, too, must have endured his share of dread, rising many mornings in a new or revisited town, knocking on strangers' doors or, perhaps worse still in his role as debt collector, knocking on doors where he'd knocked before. Selling was hard work — "it takes talking and time," as Pears describes it[15] — and travel could be cold, damp, and dirty. He missed his wife and family and they struggled without him, living in greatly reduced circumstances. Yet, his livelihood was dependent on family connections and he sorely wished to not disappoint. Under such circumstances, Pears' job must have been especially trying.

The role of men such as Pears was nearly as important in the glass industry's early years as the glass entrepreneur's. The western market for glass was wide open, developing with the new nation and changing by the day, and success demanded determined responsiveness to the dynamic market. Industrialists needed Pears and other traveling agents to constantly travel the rivers and visit the new towns as they sprouted across the countryside, for this was the only way to keep the glasshouse's products in front of retailers and to assess taste and pocketbook potential.

While the frontier's commercial structure was being stitched together, the economies of New York, Philadelphia, Baltimore, and other eastern cities supported all-purpose merchandisers and wholesalers. Merchants there also took advantage of a fairly well developed transportation system between cities. In the West, businessmen such as the Bakewells took to the rivers themselves, sensing opportunity for certain but also fearing what might happen if they delegated everything to subordinates and stayed warm and dry at home in Pittsburgh. So instructive was the traveling agent's position that some in the second generation of glasshouse owners rose to positions of leadership in their companies by learning the trade as agents.

In Pears' case, a son was also a rising star, as Bakewells & Co. became, with the ascendancy of John Pears, Bakewell & Pears in 1836. The heads of

For location of towns and factories in this chapter, see maps on page 158.

other venerable Pittsburgh companies also worked as agents: James Atterbury, first at Appleby & Hale, founded the first of several glass firms bearing his own name in the late 1850s. His internationally known concern survived until the early 20th century. Atterbury, like Pears, was related to a Bakewell, the original family glass firm which launched the careers of at least a dozen other men who climbed to industry-wide prominence by the middle of the century. As in any business empire, family connections figured heavily, but hard work on the road as a glass agent could not be beat for the experience.

The gritty lessons an agent gained would be instructive during the equally demanding years of the mid- and late 19th century. By then, Pittsburgh's own economy had come of age, with a network of wholesalers working in the city, and new ones springing up across the continent to sell Pittsburgh glass wherever the burgeoning railroad reached.

Part *II*

By the mid-19th century, technology had greatly expanded the national market and access to it. Within a very few years, further innovations, plus monumental growth and change in American life that had particular bearing on the manufacture and use of housewares, would create a mass consumer market for the products of Western Pennsylvania.

As we saw in Chapter 3, technological innovations in the manufacture of glass, as well as the use of natural gas for glasshouse furnances, had in many ways created a new industry by the 1880s. So, too, was the glass marketplace revolutionized during roughly the same period. The region's manufacturers began to specialize, not only in tablewares or housewares but also in lighting, containers, and flat glass. The wonders of electrical lighting, for example,

A frequent promotional approach was glass that could advertise itself and its maker. Higbee Co. used its cups (c. 1915) as giveaways or premiums to advertise its "sanitary" insulated "thermos" (opposite page).

were demonstrated at the Columbian Exposition in Chicago in 1893, with 250,000 Westinghouse "glass lamps" — we call them light bulbs — made in Pittsburgh. Specific niche markets and marketing strategies developed. Wholesale distribution systems established in large urban centers enabled Pittsburgh glass to reach more and more markets. New strategies for communicating with wholesalers and consumers, and new places and ways to shop, also proliferated — direct mail, trade journals, trade catalogs, new advertising outlets, and of course, the department store. Finally, by the 1880s, railroads linked producers, wholesalers, and consumers more thoroughly than ever, making a truly national market possible for the first time. Pittsburgh, at approximately the same time that it was becoming the nation's steel and glass manufacturing capital, also developed as the city where the most important decisions were made about how many sorts of glass would be marketed and sold.

The tableware industry is in many ways a special case, because the end consumers are individual purchasers, buying primarily for the home. This segment of the glass business required a different kind of marketing, sales, and distribution system than the one needed for commercial consumers, such as, for example, companies in the food and beverage industry. In tableware, Pittsburgh's importance historically as a marketing center cannot be overestimated. Beginning in the early 1880s, the nation's most prominent trade show, though small and disorganized at first, was held every January in downtown Pittsburgh. Two men, William B. Ranney, the traveling representative for Co-Operative Flint Glass Co. of Beaver County, and S.C. Dunlevy, representative for LaBelle Glass Co. of Ohio, are given credit for the show's conception. Considerable scrutiny of the show's history is justified, for the annual event provided a comprehensive picture of how glass manufacturers, wholesalers, and buyers calculated and responded to consumer trends during the industry's years of peak influence in Pittsburgh.

Mr. Ranney, disappointed by the volume of sales at his factory showroom in Beaver Falls, 35 miles northwest of Pittsburgh, decided one January to set up a display of his wares in Pittsburgh for six weeks. He reasoned that buyers visiting the showrooms of other large Pittsburgh-based companies would also see his display and place orders. The exhibit, therefore, really started as a "voluntary showing on the part of salesmen and manufacturers for the convenience of buyers."[16] The show attracted just a dozen or so buyers in its early years, but by 1889 it was fairly established, with salesman from 17 out-of-town glass factories in attendance. It became an especially important event for the region's glass tableware industry because it brought manufacturers from around Pittsburgh into contact with national buyers drawn to the showrooms of the city's dominant manufacturers. The show also enabled the industry to transform what traditionally was a down time for sales — previously, most orders were placed in the fall, before the holidays, and then again in the spring — into a boom time: the January trade show allowed buyers to preview wares for the coming year and sellers the chance to start the new year with orders in hand.

Displays were set up in the downtown hotels such the Hotel Anderson, the Hotel Neville, the Hotel Schlosser, and others. For many years, the Monongahela Hotel (considered the city's grandest, having been rebuilt after the Great Fire of 1845), located along the Monongahela River wharf across the river from Pittsburgh's South Side factories, became the show's central venue. A stop-over for dignitaries such as Abraham Lincoln and for industrialists aplenty, it became a glassman's hotel, the "Cradle of the Pittsburgh Glass Exhibit."[17]

The *Crockery and Glass Journal*, covering one of the early exhbits (1886), noted the event's increasing importance by observing that while business was slow overall, "more orders were received so far this month than in any January for several years." During the exhibit's startup years, many manufacturers feared competitors in attendance might pirate product lines displayed publicly for buyers. But by the 1890s, the show was so beneficial to the sales

Just a short walk from Pittsburgh's main passenger train station, the Fort Pitt Hotel (c. 1915) hosted the city's annual glass and ceramics trade show for over 30 years.

Fort Pitt Hotel
Pittsburg, Pa.
11336

A 573

forces of glasshouses in West Virginia, Ohio, Indiana, and those in Western Pennsylvania outside Pittsburgh that companies could not afford to miss the chance to introduce new products at the show. Few could afford to be left out of the industry's biggest annual congregation.

Surely the sales reps enjoyed having something new to offer, but the dictating of trends by the "Knights of the Grip," as one trade journal affectionately referred to salesmen, was limited. At the end of the 19th century, for example, colored glass was the rage. The *National Glass Budget*, which chose Pittsburgh as the home for its offices — further evidence of the city's importance in the trade — declared the rose pink glass of McKee & Bros., a local firm with a display at the 1899 Pittsburgh show, to be "one of the greatest achievements in colored glass ever made by an American firm."[18] Also noteworthy was the pressed glass done as an imitation of cut glass. Nonetheless, the *National Glass Budget* reporter covering the show reminded readers:

> And yet, this is all, we are free to say, a simple matter of taste and preference, which in the end may count for very little. The consumer at the end of the line, rather than the news writer and jobber or designer, decides the question of popularity, of wear well, and of sales volume. And around that one question of sale and profit, the whole thing hangs. Results decide. And prejudices and preferences count for little.[19]

Eventually the exhibit covered two full weeks, with most of the buyers from around the country and Canada present. This provided an immense savings in time and travel for people in all facets of the industry, from buyers who represented the jobbing houses that wholesaled glass to those present on behalf of the department, variety, and giftware stores. Buyers saw an incredible variety of goods — much more than any salesman could carry in his sample kit or gripsack. If salesmen were persuasive enough, a visit to the factory might be arranged, so deals and orders could be completed in private.

By 1907, the show began to shift location across town to the Fort Pitt Hotel. Located at the corner of Penn Avenue and Tenth Street downtown, the hotel was convenient to both the Pennsylvania Railroad station and to some of the established dealer showrooms. The show also began to change in focus. Pottery companies, another important industry in the Pittsburgh region historically and the other prominent wing of the houseware trade — makers of ceramic dishes, cups, saucers, and serving pieces, etc. — began to exhibit with the glass companies. By 1910, the convention was known as the

Competition in the early 20th century from a Chicago trade show led Pittsburgh manufacturers to step up advertising in trade journals such as China, Glass & Lamps *(Dec. 18, 1922). Emphasizing their advantage on the calendar, Pittsburgh organizers urged: "See it first in Pittsburgh."*

Pittsburgh Glass and Pottery Exhibit. The show's management was also reorganized, falling under direction of a manufacturer's association, the Western Glass and Pottery Association. The association was described as "a mutual benefit organization of those engaged in the production, distribution and retailing of allied wares."[20]

In 1913, 80 firms were on hand. Four years later, there were 110 exhibits in 150 rooms. More than 400 buyers attended, generating in excess of $1 million in orders.[21] It must have been an incredible scene when thousands of barrels and boxes, and dozens of harried salesmen descended on downtown Pittsburgh. Amidst a flurry of unpacking, paper and straw strewn about, the hotel hallways clogged with barrels so tightly that people could hardly pass; the smoke and the noise and the possibilities that awaited! Then the first buyers arrived on the scene, order books in hand. One year, a near-disaster broke the tension:

GIRL SMASHES $300 WORTH OF CUT GLASS

One of the maids at the Hotel Henry, Pittsburg, while cleaning the room of Val Bergen, pushed a Morris chair under one of the display tables, knocked a "horse" from under it and sent sixteen rich cut glass vases and a number of small pieces crashing to the floor. In trying to catch the falling board the girl bumped into another table and broke more pieces. The loss, which was placed at $300, was promptly made good by the hotel.[22]

Of course, that was why the show existed in part: each year, thousands bought glass and thousands more broke it.

Above: The Pittsburgh trade show was so important that companies teased buyers with ads that previewed new lines to be introduced at the show. Right: Glass manufacturers, meanwhile, continually sought new consumers with items like this miniature homemaker's set (c. 1940) packaged and sold to children.

By 1920, remarked the *National Glass Budget*, "Buyers are placing large orders and seem to appreciate this annual event more now than ever .... They can accomplish as much in two days by attending the show as it would be possible for them to do in two weeks' time, if they had to call at the different manufacturing plants."[23] As was true in many industries where trade shows had grown in stature, buyers had the chance to compare ware and prices before placing any orders. Salesman could display their staples and premier new lines. And manufacturers could judge what was going to sell in the coming year before committing to large-scale production.

The show worked so well that it attracted competition. In 1921, the trade journals announced a competing show in Chicago. Home to the growing housewares industry no longer dominated as much by glass objects, and conveniently located in the center of the country with rail links to everywhere, a show in Chicago represented serious competition.

Organizers of the Pittsburgh show responded to this threat in several ways. They formed a new association, the Associated Glass and Pottery Manufacturers, and they stepped up advertising to the trade, running full-page ads in the journals below a new slogan, "See it first in Pittsburgh." Pittsburgh organizers saw advantage in remaining the first show of the year — the Chicago show was set for two weeks in February — so their advertising also urged buyers and sellers to "start the new year right, be in Pittsburgh in January."

Through the 1920s, such a theme seemed to work. *China, Glass & Lamps* reported in 1924 that about one-quarter of the year's new business, some $40 million, was done in Pittsburgh in January.[24] Of course, at the same time the exhibit at the Congress Hotel and nearby showrooms in Chicago touted its success at attracting more than 2,000 buyers. Still, calendar position favored Pittsburgh, for it was said that what was new was new first in Pittsburgh.

As part of each year's show, a dinner attended by all salesmen helped to knit the organization together socially. The dinners became elaborate affairs, reported on with gusto in the trade journals. Often held in locations around town other than the hotels, the banquets provided an opportunity for local members of the manufacturers association to fete out-of-town colleagues. Their efforts did not, however, always meet with great success. The 1922 banquet, held in the dining room of Kaufmann's department store downtown, trumpeted a multi-course menu sure to please "the most critical taste." Entertainment included the band from the H.C. Fry Glass Co. of Rochester, in their "natty uniforms."[25] However, the banquet was "not what might be termed a great success, either from the standpoint of attendance or entertainment."[26] In the opinion of the influential *National Glass Budget*, more atten-

McKee Glass' "Bottoms-Up and Bottoms-Down" tumbler and mug (c. 1935) cleverly couples the popular motif of a nude form with the slang associated with imbibing.

tion should have been paid to reporting on current business conditions and to suggestions for advancing the trade.

The organization and presentation of wares at the show began to change in the 1930s. Trade shows had become big business, and had begun to rely on both industrial designers and exhibit display manufacturers who provided a more polished look to the displays, most of which were set up in a battery of hotel rooms and adjoining suites. The Gardner Sign Co. of Pittsburgh was one such company that sold portable display units with built-in signage that could also be used for window displays in retailers' stores. Glass companies also began making retailers' signs in glass that could be displayed with the glass company's product line in the stores, to aid in the development of brand name recognition by the consumer. A flurry of trade journal articles endeavored to educate manufacturers and buyers about the use of display techniques to increase visibility and sales.

The Pittsburgh show shifted in location again from the Fort Pitt Hotel to the William Penn Hotel, which in 1929 had expanded on the Grant Street side. The hotel had more large rooms, such as the "Urban Room," to accommodate expanded displays and booths. By this time, the Pittsburgh show was not only competing with the Chicago exhibit but also with permanent merchandise marts, such as the one built in Chicago in 1930. A brand new skyscraper, with 4 million feet of display space, it had two floors devoted just to glass and lamps. In addition, all housewares — furniture, appliances, china, and dinnerware — could be found, allowing one-stop shopping for buyers. "The Mart" was open year-round, with many new lines installed in February to coincide with the Chicago exhibit.

The building of such merchandise marts completely changed the way glass and china were presented to wholesalers and forever altered the structure of the buying season, too. In marts or exhibition halls, buyers could see the wares of many more companies, often on one floor, even in one large room. The hotel room shows pioneered in Pittsburgh obviously were more cramped. Of course, while exhibition halls afforded increased visibility, they also afforded little privacy for companies placing orders: every salesmen knew when the buyers for big concerns entered the hall, and such buyers' every move was watched. Nonetheless, the new won out. The Pittsburgh show, which had been suspended during the peak years of World War II, gradually diminished in importance. Trade events in New York and then Atlantic City, combined with the building of merchandise marts around the country, reverberated with a death knell for Pittsburgh's 70-odd year domination of glassware marketing.

Changes behind the scenes in retailing also had an important impact on the selling of glass. Recognizing the salesperson as the vital link between fac-

During Prohibition, when cocktails made bootleg liquor palatable, glassmakers introduced new bar ware. Opposite page: McKee Glass, "Lifesaver" decanter and shot glass and, above, McKee's "Jolly Golfer" decanter and tumblers.

Above: A page from Pittsburgh Plate Glass' 1923 yearbook shows the variety of goods it made and distributed. Below: Many companies use glass containers because consumers are known to believe it is more sanitary (Heinz jars, 1929-1955). Mothers buy it for the baby food, but the glass packaging creates a subtle positive association for Heinz.

tory and consumer, retail managers and proprietors began placing an increased emphasis on the preparation of salespeople during the first three decades of the 20th century. Many educational texts and training programs were developed. One such program was the Research Bureau for Retail Training housed at the University of Pittsburgh and funded by seven local department stores. In 1925, as part of a series of *Merchandise Manuals for Retail Salespeople,* the Pitt program produced a text on china and glassware. "The manuals have been prepared as text-books for salespeople and as reference books for buyers, assistant buyers, department coaches, and teachers in training departments."[27] Salespeople were advised that if they "read the manual conscientiously and then answer the test questions, doing what is suggested in each one, you can not help becoming a more intelligent and useful salesperson."[28]

Creative retailing, largely independent of the glass industry, stimulated demand for glassware during the past century as gift merchandise for special occasions. Bridal registries, for instance, created demand for crystal and other fine glass for new homes and lives. Traditional glass bowls for serving fruit, in particular, became so popular that they were known as "bridal baskets." Some glass manufacturers capitalized by issuing a series of glass baskets with handles used for floral arrangements, candy, nuts, and of course, brides. Today there is a large market in holiday glassware, especially Christmas ware. Companies such as Lenox in Westmoreland County produce and package holiday glassware that coordinates china, Lenox glassware, and table linens. The combinations are then advertised by department stores and gift shops, and in direct mail catalogs.

In contrast, sales forces in the other branches of the industry — flat glass, containers, and industrial glass — conduct their business with companies and

a little extra glass means a lot of extra charm

The huge upswing in home ownership after World War II led glass manufacturers known more for industrial products, such as Pittsburgh Plate Glass (brochure, 1950), to approach homeowners directly with the wide diversity of its business.

corporations that use or repackage glass in their products. Sales agents in those branches do not typically meet the end-consumer. In the flat glass and container market, for example, glass is usually one part of a final product: with a new home or a car, the windows are included; with beer or soda or ketchup, the container is part of the product, and the individual consumer doesn't choose the sort of window used, or the color of the bottle. Someone else has made the decision about the glass in those items — an architect, industrial designer, builder, or bottler. Therefore, much of the marketing of such products is handled differently than in the marketing of glass for houseware items.

Specific vehicles for marketing to the trade developed in the late 19th and early 20th centuries. Publications, specifically *Sweet's Indexed Catalogue of Building Construction*, and journals such as *Architectural Record* provided an organized compendium for the buyers of architectural glass. Flat glass manufacturers also advertised in glass trade journals likely to be used by their clientele, such as the *National Glass Budget*. It provided thorough analysis of all branches of the business, as well as information on patents, machinery, raw materials, sales, and systems of distribution. The journal also published a yearly directory listing all the glass manufacturers in the country, their size, and their products.

Like tableware manufacturers, flat glass makers also used service associations to educate the trade and to serve as vehicles for marketing their products. In 1936, the Pittsburgh Glass Institute was founded to serve as "an authoritative agency to which architects and other members of the building industry may resort for information on the increasingly versatile uses of glass as a construction and decorative material."[29] Though founded by Pittsburgh glass companies, the institute chose Rockefeller Plaza in New York City, the nation's marketing center, as its headquarters. The institute assembled and disseminated information on new products and their applications. The flood

of new architectural glass materials developed in the 20th century — glass block, safety glass, and structural glass such as the opaque glass resembling marble which Pittsburgh Plate Glass marketed as "Cararra glass" — required technical instruction for architects and builders who wished to use such glass products in their projects.

Many companies devoted millions in marketing resources to keep their names and products at the center of the trade. PPG, for instance, in 1923 published a yearbook that served as an excellent sales tool. The book provided a history of glass and glassmaking, as well as a history of the company, while the liberally illustrated text detailed the PPG product line and the workings of its national distribution network.

With new types of glass or new uses for glass (reamers, above, c. 1930, or the heat resistant meat platter, below, c. 1920), came the need to stimulate demand through "educational" campaigns. This was especially true in kitchenware, where companies spent millions to allay consumers' fear of breakage.

Black-and-white photographs documented production and the workforce. More elaborate than a catalog, the book provided a polished, professional image of the corporation that bespoke longevity, inventiveness, and quality. In the period following World War II, PPG also developed a series of publications to inform the growing mass of new homeowners about PPG glass products for the home; pamphlets and booklets dealt with such topics as decorating with mirrors and integrating glass into kitchen and bathroom designs.

A few companies had been doing such direct-to-the consumer marketing

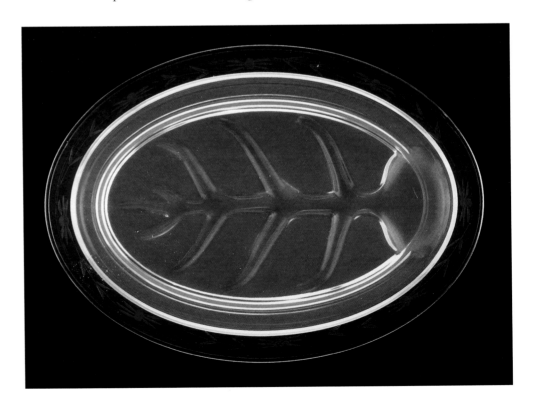

for many years. When George Macbeth developed his patented "Pearl Top" lamp chimneys in 1883, he secured trademarks for them and began to advertise them by name. (Establishment of the U.S. Trade Mark office in 1870 offered manufacturers the opportunity to develop exclusive brand-name recognition of their products.) Protected by design patents and trademark status, Macbeth moved to share the Pearl Top chimney with the buying public. He contracted with a St. Louis advertising agency and spent $25,000 in his first year. Three years later, in 1886, he signed John Powers as his ad man and together they developed a campaign that made extensive use of direct marketing techniques such as car cards for the New York Elevated Railways. Using language that was considered direct for the times, Macbeth exhorted, "One chimney a year is enough for a lamp, if you get the right chimney. Macbeth."[30]

Jeannette Glass' jaunty hat (c. 1930) was a retail display piece — intended to grab attention and increase brand recognition for the company's consumer glass products.

Macbeth also advertised in the popular magazines of the day, including *Pictorial Review*. Other companies — the H.C. Fry Glass Co., Duncan Miller, and McKee — bought space in women's magazines such as *Ladies Home Journal*. Launching new product lines such as glass ovenware required an extensive consumer education campaign. Two of the companies with glass ovenware lines, Fry and McKee, used ads in women's magazines to persuade women not to be afraid of cooking in glass. In addition, the companies offered recipes and cookbooks that required new, specialized pieces of ovenware.

New forms of glass tableware were often marketed the same way. When industrial-scale refrigeration made the long distance shipment of citrus fruits possible, glass reamers or juicers were often marketed in the ads for fruits or fruit juices. Reamers produced by McKee Glass appeared in the Sunkist ads, and the fruit company also used the reamers emblazoned with its logo as sales premiums.

Technological and social change in the middle third of the 20th century even brought glassmakers that previously sold almost exclusively to other industial buyers into direct contact with consumers at the "street level." The Great Depression of the 1930s halted the commercial building boom of the century's early decades, forcing makers of large plate and window glass to aggressively pursue new markets. A few companies took advantage of new communications technologies. Pittsburgh Plate Glass in 1936 turned to radio, linking its name to the ideals of quality and culture through sponsorship of national broadcasts of the Pittsburgh Symphony Orchestra on the National Broadcasting Company network.[31] The Pittsburgh glassmaker took its Carrara glass line, first developed as a glass for ornamental and highly specialized sanitary surfaces, to new heights. As we shall see in Chapter 5, Carrara found wide application on America's Main Street as a sleek, machine-age renovation material. Glass block for windows are a related innovation.

The Duncan Miller Glass Co. of Washington, Pennsylvania, meanwhile, chose the big screen. Perhaps senior citizens among us remember the glass company's display in stores which boasted, "The lovely Ginger Rogers uses the lovely Duncan glass in 'Swing Time'."[32] The company got good mileage out of such sponsorship: a September 1936 *New Yorker* article explained that

Duncan Miller had been chosen exclusive provider of "lovely glassware" for RKO movies.

Of continuing importance for the marketing of glass were large fairs and expositions. As noted in Chapter 1, the J.B. Lyon Co. of Pittsburgh earned acclaim at international fairs as early as 1867, when it displayed its pressed glass at a Paris exposition. Marking the American centennial in 1876 was another popular exposition in which more than 10 million people marveled at products from 47 American glassmakers. Similarly, the 1939 World's Fair included a "Glass Center" built and sponsored by the Corning Glass Works, Pittsburgh Plate Glass, and the Owens-Illinois Glass Co. Visitors entered a huge rotunda with mirrored ceilings to find an exhibition on the 5,000-year history of glass, a working furnace, technical demonstrations, examples of new products, and a section titled, "Glass in the Home." Glass furniture, mirrors, and heat resistant glass kitchenware were among the breakthroughs on display.

Glass companies still use and benefit from diverse media. The L.E. Smith Glass Co. of Mt. Pleasant, Pennsylvania, reaped unexpected fortunes in the mid-1990s from a Martha Stewart television segment. Demonstrating a new use for an old piece, America's favorite domestic stylemaker set a Thanksgiving table with the colorless, covered turkey-shaped dishes that L.E. Smith made decades earlier. Using the turkey dishes as soup bowls, Stewart intoned, was a good thing. L.E. Smith couldn't agree more. The company reissued the piece, and its national sales manager travelled the country with turkeys in tow, setting Thanksgiving tables in countless showrooms just as Stewart had. Sales were so successful that in 1997, the company made plans to produce a covered soup bowl for everyday use.

The episode illustrates particularly well how consumer perception has influenced marketing, form, and function in the glass industry. For more than 200 years, glass manufacturers — a large percentage of them Pittsburgh companies — have successfully capitalized on trends in a society where change often seems the only constant. Glass, a miracle material, so fragile, perhaps also possesses the property of eternal youth.

Marketing and design intersect frequently in the glass business. When designers at Fry Glass Co. recongized the attractive color and quality of its ovenware glass, they developed a houseware line (FOVAL, or Fry Oven Art Glass) that included a rare radiowave lamp (c. 1930). Opposite page: When one design sells well, manufacturers often introduce similar or complementary pieces. When homemaker icon Martha Stewart adapted L.E. Smith's turkey bowl for holiday soups (1997), the Mt. Pleasant, Pa., company immediately introduced the "Alexander Egg" bowl for everyday use.

CHAPTER

Design

Glass designers rely on the world around them for ideas. Cubist art inspired Reuben Haley's design for the "Ruba Rombic" decanter set, made at Consolidated Lamp & Glass of Coraopolis, Pa., c. 1930. Whether it be stained glass windows (opposite page, watercolor study by Rudy Bros. Studio of Pittsburgh, c. 1925) or whiskey glasses, their design reveals much about American life and the times in which the objects were conceived.

Rising to dominance of the nation's glass industry during the Industrial Revolution had profound implications not only for how Pittsburgh glass was manufactured, marketed, and distributed, but also for how it was designed. The word "design" derives from the Latin root "*designare*," meaning "to mark out, define," and nearly all manufactured objects start as concepts. Design is a purposeful activity. Before the first of a particular style or type of manufactured object emerges from the factory, it is coddled conceptually for dozens of hours — sometimes months or years — so that its form, function, aesthetics, and likely acceptance in the marketplace may be calculated.

Glass is no different, and Pittsburgh's companies, which, as we have seen in previous chapters may attribute their ascendancy in the industry largely to a knack for exploiting technological changes, showed a comparable flair for design. During the last half of the 19th century and continuing well into the 20th century, Pittsburgh specialized in designing glassware that appealed in form, ornamentation, function, and price to the nation's emerging middle and upper-middle classes. But not only was the city a hub of glass design. When popular lines of glassware were introduced elsewhere, Pittsburghers often demonstrated a genius for adapting them to factory production on a massive scale, at unbeatable prices.

Related to those achievements was the mastering of glassmaking's chemistry; we shall see that in this realm, too, Pittsburgh firms excelled, turning out a rainbow of colors consistent from one industrial-sized batch to the next. Such control in the manufacturing process — again, allied with cost-cutting technologies — enabled designers to further broaden the appeal of fashionable styles and forms by making them available in colors intended to suit any consumer's fancy.

Glass objects may be designed to be utilitarian, or as pieces of art. Designers bring their own cultural interpretations to their task, and individual associations shape the conception, the creation, and the understanding of any manufactured object. Time also alters our understanding of purpose. Something utilitarian — a pitcher, tumbler, or vase — may develop symbolic associations so potent that we stop using the piece, setting it aside to prevent its loss or destruction. Artists, meanwhile, are quick to point out the utility of veneration: appreciation of an object purely because its appearance delights us bestows utility — meaning, usefulness — in the same way that a pitcher, vase, or tumbler has functional utility. Examining design in glassmaking uncovers the complex relationship between manufacturer, use, and user.

In the glass industry's earliest days in Western Pennsylvania, the person who conceived of a glass object also usually manufactured it. So long as artisanship dominated society's commercial structure, the designer and the maker were one — or, at the very least the craftsman, if he were not the glasshouse owner, worked closely with the owner and perhaps the firm's traveling agent (who had direct contact with customer demands and competing firms) in designing the objects to be made. Most glassmakers at Gallatin's and O'Hara's works, for instance, gained training in the artisanal system abroad, in the glassmaking traditions of England and Germany. O'Hara's black porter bottles were virtually identical

Popular designs are often copied. In 1928, just two months after Consolidated premiered Ruba Rombic (previous page), Kopp Glass of Swissvale, Pa., introduced its Modernistic line — including this lamp.

to counterparts in Britain, while the window glass that Gallatin's blowers made by the cylinder method borrowed from Europe was so similar that it was referred to as "German glass."

Having been trained within the artisan system rather than at a technical school or university, artisan glassmakers typically had a limited knowledge of chemistry, although formulas for making certain kinds of glass were well-known. As a result, their control of color in the works' glass was inconsistent; nature — the trace elements and impurities in the raw materials, particularly in the sand — usually determined color. Additionally, product lines were controlled by furnace design and whatever tools and molds were used commonly in the shop. Glasshouses often turned away designs not done "in-house." O'Hara in 1809, for instance, elects not to manufacture an item brought to him because his blowers were "apprehensive that they cannot please in accuracy. [T]he patterns will be returned...."[1]

Ornamentation was another area in which stylistic traditions and the training of workers figured heavily during the early era of American glass. The accounts of factory visits and comments in the press underscore this view. "Mr. Bakewell's works are admirable," observed Elias Fordham in 1817. "He has excellent artists, both French and English. His cut glass equals the best I have ever seen in England."[2] Anne Royall, on visiting the Bakewell works in 1828, commented similarly on the engraving: "The patterns are mostly obtained from Europe, and the patterns executed, ... for beauty and taste were exquisite, particularly a *grey-hound*."[3]

Alex Jardelle, an engraver at Bakewell's whose skills were critical to the company's product designs, was from France, and it was in France that Tom Pears, whose company travels were covered extensively in Chapter 3, searched for additional cutters and engravers in 1816 and again in 1818. Jardelle had been with Bakewell's for at least 12 years by the time Anne

A tiny salt dish made by Stourbridge Flint Glass Works of Pittsburgh (c. 1830), just 3 inches long, documents the period when steamboats built in Western Pennsylvania traversed the inland rivers loaded with Pittsburgh products.

Royall visited the factory, but his stylistic repertoire dated from the earlier period in which he had gained his training.[4] Pittsburgh factories that produced fine wares had stiff competition from imported glass. Most firms found that survival meant concentrating on the familiar and popular.

Depending on the client, design also incorporated the iconography of the emerging American consciousness. This is evident in the glass Bakewell's produced for the White House. Glass made for both James Madison and Andrew Jackson was engraved with decoration that integrated elements from the Great Seal of the United States. Especially popular in the iconography celebrating the young republic's national government was the bald eagle (with a central shield on Madison's glass, and standing triumphant on a shield on Jackson's). Additions of 13 stars, a banner, an olive branch, and arrows integrated other symbols of America into the decoration of the two sets of presidential glass.[5] Such symbols resonated so strongly with consumers that even glass produced abroad for the American market was adorned with eagles and other patriotic images.

During this period, a vocabulary of design that may be considered particularly "American," especially in ornamentation, began to be articulated; the articulation accelerated after the invention of pressing in 1826, once again highlighting the critical link between technical innovation and design in American glass. As previously discussed, early pressed glass or "lacy" glass used an all-over design to mask imperfections that resulted from a lack of control of the molding technique. While Pittsburgh examples of lacy glass reveal classical motifs such as Gothic arches, and show the continuing influence of European design by borrowing patterns such as the strawberry diamond design from cut glass, many examples also include symbols of the American republic and its commercial achievements. Another familiar design element in Pittsburgh pressed glass was the company's own name, which allowed glassmakers to trumpet their skill and imagination.

Similarly, mold-blown bottles, such as figural and historical flasks manufactured widely until approximately 1875, typically displayed "American" motifs in recognition of major events and individuals in the 19th century. Relief patterning on the glass surface depicted the great men of the nation (George Washington or Andrew Jackson), the industriousness of Americans (sheaves of grain or overflowing cornucopias), and political achievements (the 13 stars of the original colonies). Frequently the designs integrated a factory name, such as "Wm. Ihmsen" on the firm's agricultural flask, or "John Taylor" on the flask made at his Brownsville factory in 1828 as a campaign piece for John Q. Adams. Sometimes only initials were used, such as "J.R. &

Son" for glassmaker John Robinson. Often "Pittsburgh" or "Pittsburgh glass" also appeared, sometimes in an oval on the lower body of the piece. The maker's name or a geographical reference allowed consumers to showcase their desire to own pieces made in America. Motifs that resonated with pride and patriotism were coupled with messages that encouraged the purchase of the young nation's products.

The machinery and metal molds required for making pressed glass also affected who made design decisions in the glasshouse. Individuals with skills never before needed — mold-makers, machinists, and metal workers — ascended rapidly to positions of great importance in the company, for their technical skills were essential to product design. The mold-maker, not the glassmaker or ornamenter, created the iron form that determined the object's shape and surface. As the machinists and metal workers who jammed Pittsburgh's streets gained familiarity with glass molds and how glass and metal interacted, the intricacy and complexity of pressed glass patterns quickly improved. In 10 years, by the mid-1830s, molds were available with detailed patterns: rondels, arches, acanthus, oak leaves, and miniature boats with intricate touches such as anchors and ropes.

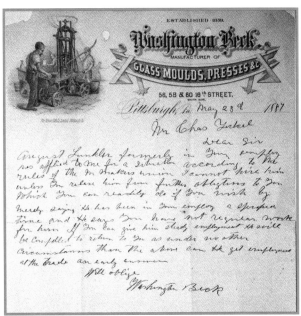

Glass and mold-makers also capitalized on the essential characteristics of the medium with which they worked. Pressed glass borrowed heavily from cut glass, and by the 1840s and '50s, simple geometric designs that accentuated the reflective quality of the piece predominated. For instance, the all-over ovals of the Argus pattern transformed a glass compote into pools of shimmering rainbows, each oval like a mirror. Placed in a shopkeeper's window where it caught the sunlight, these pieces must have sold themselves. With the expressive use of panels, flutes, and ovals, pressed patterns replicated simple cut-glass decoration in style and effect. The replicating of cut-glass in pressed glass continued: at the turn of the 20th century, many pressed glass patterns mimicked the heavy cut glass (called "rich-cut") of the day. Marketed by McKee of Jeannette as "Prescut" and by Cambridge Glass in Ohio as "Nearcut," these less expensive substitutes for real cut glass found a ready market.

Pittsburgh metal workers and mold-makers developed an especially broad vocabulary in glass design due to the presence in the region of several emerging industries which also used standardized patterns. The makers of cast iron, tin, bronze, brass, and silver, plus cabinet makers and carpentry shops, and the printing and textile trades, often consulted the same mold and

Opposite page: In choosing a common patriotic motif for its cup plate (c. 1835), the Fort Pitt Glass Works created a positive association for the company that also encouraged consumers to "buy American." Above: Pressing technology opened new realms in design and made mold makers such as Pittsburgh's Washington Beck important figures in the creation of glass.

commercial pattern books, catalogs, and trade materials. In addition, popular magazines and travel literature, and the imported goods readily available in large U.S. cities by this time, clearly affected designers for industry, just as the larger population was influenced in matters of style and fashion. What's more, craftsmen who migrated to the city from the east — silversmiths such as Andrew Osthoff from Baltimore, or the pianoforte maker Charles Rosenbaum — produced pieces for their Pittsburgh clients contemporary in style and pattern with what could be purchased in Philadelphia or Baltimore. As early as 1801, Greensburg cabinet maker Samuel Davis proclaimed in an ad that he had experience "in different parts of the United States, and practiced with European workmen," and could build "any fashion of Walnut or Cherry Furniture, either ornamented or plain."[6]

A striking example of the cross-fertilization going on in design is that the same patterns of inlay that ornamented Western Pennsylvania furniture are found on pressed glass made in the region during the period. Vines and leaves, hearts, pinwheels, and rondels were translated into glass patterns, and given names such as Sprig, Bellflower, Roman Rosette, and Band. As mechanics became more adept with complex motifs, they also carved molds that included elements of classical ornamentation in the glass form. Candlestick and compote stems shaped like dolphins, for example, were coordinated with other decorative elements in Empire-style furniture and cast iron stoves.

Glass for use in the home, especially in the early 19th century, was coordinated with other decorative elements of a room. Silver, ceramics, furniture, fabrics, even the cast iron stove, often shared a vocabulary of contemporary form and pattern. Women sought to create interiors of decorative harmony that connected one room to the next. It makes sense, then, that glass designers became great "copyists" and that Pittsburgh designers, producing by the mid-19th century for a mass market, would borrow freely and widely from other fine and decorative arts.

Among the most copied designs were those of competing glassmakers. Deming Jarves of Boston kept abreast of what his chief competitors, fine tableware producers such as Bakewell's or John Robinson, were manufacturing in Pittsburgh, and vice-versa. What sold well in the 1850s and '60s for one glasshouse was likely to be tried by another; many popular patterns were made and sold over the course of several decades. The glassware pattern now popularly known as Loop, to cite but one example, was produced at several factories in Pittsburgh, Wheeling, Boston, Portland, Maine, and possibly Canada, and was marketed under a multitude of names. Makers and designers increasingly turned to the use of patents or licensing to protect their handiwork. Makers also sought to develop and protect the markets for their glass by using names with geographical references. Company names for patterns of glass, such as "New York" or "Cincinnati" for a honeycomb pattern, had less to do with design than with the belief that the name would bestow a cachet for capturing a niche market. As leaders in the industry nationally, Pittsburgh's glass companies were in the enviable position of not having to look hundreds of miles away for all their inspiration: they could borrow ideas from chief competitors whose headquarters often were located right down the street.

Events and trends in American life also played an increasingly important role in the design of glass for home use. By the mid-19th century, the home was seen as a sanctuary from the outside world and as a realm in which women presided, symbolizing in their decorating selections the family's values and morals. Religious literature and advice manuals for women reinforced the notion of home as a refuge and sanctuary. One Christian tract intoned that

> one of the holiest sanctuaries on earth is home. The family altar is
> more venerable than any altar in the cathedral. The education of the
> soul for eternity begins by the fireside. The principle of love, which is
> to be carried through the universe, is first unfolded in the family.[7]

Religious artifacts, produced for home use, became a way to both sanctify domestic space and demonstrate in a material way one's commitment to God. Women were instructed on creating a home space that was morally uplifting, supportive, and restorative. One means of achieving this aim was to surround oneself with religious objects and images. By the late 1840s, "Parian" ware manufacturers in England were producing religious statuary for home use,

Glass designers stayed abreast of trends in home design, as shown by this parlor scene (c. 1895). Note how the table lamp, especially, is coordinated with other aspects of the room's interior design.

and within 10 years, similar items were made by the United States Pottery Co. in Bennington, Vermont.[8] Lithographs and painted images of a religious nature, especially of the Madonna and Child (glorifying both God and mother) became popular wall ornamentation. Glassmakers followed the trend. A variety of overtly religious glass objects were designed and made in the mid- to late 19th century such as candlesticks in the shape of the cross. Other spiritual efforts were more subtle. Ripley & Co. made a series of lamps with religious iconography as decoration that were later named for those rites of passage associated with religious ceremony. Among those styles are "baptismal" and "marriage" lamps.

Religious symbols and sayings also decorated pieces of tableware already vested with ceremonial meaning, such as bread plates. One such plate, the "Rock of Ages" platter produced by Atterbury, had a large cross in the center with two female figures below. "Give us this day our daily bread" surrounded the image. Other plates had the Last Supper or faith, hope, and charity as design themes. Compotes and stemmed tableware also integrated biblical stories or figures. For instance, Bakewell, Pears & Co. produced a compote with a woman carrying water — Rebecca at the Well — as the stem. Praying hands or "Crucifix" glassware drew upon a multitude of Christian symbols. This glass was carried in trade catalogs and marketed along with secular (that is, non-religious) patterns. Glass objects with religious themes were marketed to women, who were the exclusive consumers of goods for the home, for their creations of the "domestic altar."

Architectural glass of the mid- to late 19th century, like glass for domestic use and display, also reflected the secularization of church and the sanctification of home. A much wider variety was available for windows, which in past times were simple and utilitarian — transparent vehicles for admitting light and providing protection from the elements. Leaded and stained glass windows, previously used primarily in churches, became part of the architectural vocabulary of schools, public buildings, factories, and homes. Because of their traditional association with churches, such windows symbolized morality and religious education. A popular accent element of Gothic Revival architecture, residential windows by their very shape in the mid-19th century visually represented links between church building and home space.

Using a decorative palette of color, texture, pattern, and paint, images created in such windows advanced their symbolic relevance. Many of the window "scenes" told stories or taught lessons, commemorated an event, or honored the home's owners. The library window of H.J. Heinz's Pittsburgh home, Greenlawn, recalled his German heritage in its recreation of the ancestral Heinz home. Some windows celebrated the role of the home as the site of

Local companies made religious glassware for the home, such as candlesticks (c. 1870) and crucifix lamps (c. 1920), well into the 20th century. Their display demonstrated in Victorian America the household's commitment to God.

For location of towns and factories in this chapter, see maps on page 158.

moral education — using literary figures or parables as illustrations. Sometimes the stained glass patterns simply enhanced or announced a room and its function, such as fruit baskets adorning dining room windows. Understanding the intended meaning of windows often required a knowledge of religious imagery, literature, or even the language of flowers. Or, meaning was often more obvious. The windows executed for the Heinz plant in Allegheny City (Pittsburgh's North Side today) by the Rudy Brothers Studio, whose Pittsburgh offices were in the Highland Park area, were boldly instructive. Morals such as "Luck may help a man over a ditch if he jumps well" appeared under the imagery on the stained glass.

In addition, stained and leaded glass windows became important decorative elements in the Victorian aesthetic in home design and ornamentation. Victorian sensibilities dwelt in rich colors and textures, in fabrics and textiles, furniture, and wall coverings. Designers liked to integrate exterior paint and woodgrain colors and patterns with interior architectural details, stonework, and metal hardware and adornment. Much like the crazy quilts, decorative embroidery, or patterned upholstery that adorned public spaces in the home, the rich colors, textures, and interplay of light, color, and patterns offered by stained glass windows were prized. Not only does stained glass provide a degree of privacy and, yet, transparency, but it also serves a decorative function, ever-changing as the natural light shifts during the day.

Stained glass studios flourished in Pittsburgh in the late 19th and early 20th centuries. As immigrants flooded in to fill jobs in the booming steel, glass, electrical, and coal industries, they carved out ethnic neighborhoods and eventually built churches and other civic institutions, providing business across the region for the city's studios. Meanwhile, the expanding economy also created a middle class of professionals, doctors, lawyers, and bankers, and business managers such as accountants and salesmen. New city neighborhoods such as the East End, and outside the city, in the South Hills, developed as favorites of the new professionals. Stained glass was an important architectural element in new homes, schools, and businesses built around the turn of the century.

In tracking commissions by the Rudy Brothers in the first decade of the 1900s, clear patterns emerge. Their clients tended to be clustered near their East End studio in the neighborhoods of Shadyside, Oakland, Squirrel Hill, Friendship, Highland Park, and Point Breeze. The list of occupations of those

for whom the Rudy company worked reads like a litany of the new manageri-
al and middle class: broker, pay master, physician, lawyer, superintendent,
dentist, doctor, and so on.[9] The expanding middle class, with its various commercial and community connections, proved lucrative for the Rudy Brothers
and other stained glass specialists, such as Pittsburgh Stained Glass Studio.

Important political, social, and cultural events of the 19th and 20th centuries also continued to influence design. Both the Civil War and the Spanish
American War were commemorated on bottles and flasks, glass novelties, and
tableware. The nation's 1876 Centennial not only spawned a plethora of

objects adorned with images of the Liberty Bell,
Centennial Hall, and other patriotic motifs, but also
revived an interest in classical form. The gift of the
Statue of Liberty from the French to the American
people in 1884 spawned a wealth of objects with
stems depicting fully figured, classical women and
classical heads and faces.

Even political campaigns, political figures, and
the death of political leaders inspired design.
Historical flasks and the ceramic plaques at the bottom of sulphide tumblers carried the profiles of
George Washington, French leader Lafayette, or New York Governor DeWitt
Clinton. Men such as President William McKinley were immortalized in glass
after his assassination. Popular figures of the day,
including women, were also rendered; both singer
Jenny Lind and newspaper writer Nellie Bly were cast
in glass. Bly appeared on a platter clutching her suitcase,
fully dressed for her trip around the world. Seminal events
were also portrayed, sometimes subtly. The laying of the
transatlantic communications cable inspired a multitude of designs
that integrated a cable motif. If an event, person, or idea was popular, if it
made news or touched hearts, some aspect of it was sure to appear in
glass.

Mastery of the pressing process also allowed for a proliferation of glass
forms and patterns. New glass forms were introduced, cake baskets and
bread plates among them, and familiar forms such as nappies (small
bowls) were made in a multitude of sizes, each with a specialized use.
Nappies were was also marketed as items to be used in a variety of
ways. Another example, of special merit due to its popularity among
Pittsburgh manufacturers, was the pitcher. Although pitchers had
been made for decades in the region, the temperance movement

By the late 19th century,
stained glass studios in
Pittsburgh such as those of
J. Horace Rudy, left (c. 1900),
were designing for churches and
other religious buildings, as well
as for homes and public
buildings. The Rudy firm's
watercolor illustration for an
angel glass window, opposite
page, dates from about 1920.
Below: Popular interest in the
classical arts may well have
influenced the Crystal Glass
Co.'s redesign of its compote
(c. 1880) to include the
classical figure as the stem.

that began in the late 19th century dramatically increased demand for water and citrus drinks as non-alcoholic alternatives. The result was pitchers packaged with tumblers and sold as water, lemonade, and iced tea "sets." These sets remained popular through Prohibition. "Lemonade sets form one of the most popular creations of colored glass," remarked one trade journal, "and so many of them are made every year [that] one cannot but wonder what becomes of them all."[10]

By contrast, during Prohibition in the 1920s and early '30s, there was an explosion in the consumption of alcoholic cocktails — mixers helping to mask the low-quality of bootlegged liquor — that led to lines of specialized bar ware: martini glasses, cocktail shakers, Old Fashioned and whisky sour glasses — the list goes on. More recently, daiquiri and margarita glasses have served the same specialty market.

Developed as containers for condiments and as serving pieces, glass animals made in the region (1880-1895) recall in design and color earlier ceramic forms.

Part II

Coinciding with demands for new applications of glass, beginning in the mid-19th century, and especially apparent in consumer products for the home, were the many important technical advances in glass manufacturing which were discussed in Chapter 3. Coincidences in commerce occur less by happenstance than meets the eye, for innovators many times are driven by the knowledge that they are working in a field of industry where demand is already established. Although risk of failure is always high, the rewards for success in a thriving industry were likely to be very lucrative.

And so we have seen how, in glass, revolutionary technical achievements took place while activity across the industry was humming. As countless new applications for glass were being discovered, as new efficiencies and cost-savings in manufacturing were constantly being applied, as tremendous changes were occurring in how glass was being advertised, marketed, and distributed (analyzed in Chapter 4), designers of glass products were working overtime also.

A striking example of this sort of industrial synergy revolves around the 1864 invention of the soda lime formula by William Leighton, Sr. (an innovation detailed in Chapter 3). Leighton substituted the common material soda lime for expensive lead in the mix of raw materials that produces colorless "flint" glass. Using Leighton's formula, factories across the region and the nation introduced a glass similar in weight and clarity to leaded glass, but at far less expense. So strong was the allure of flint glass in the marketplace that, prior to Leighton's innovation, the absence of color in glass was considered a sign of superior quality. Chemical impurities in the sand used as a raw material were responsible primarily for the greens and blues of utilitarian glass objects of the early to mid-19th century. There, color was largely accidental.

Not all colored glass was accidental, however, and Pittsburgh's reputation for quality and artistic excellence owed much to the leaded glass and the bold colored glass of a few firms. Creating color in the finished product required an understanding of chemistry — knowing what chemical constituents in the raw materials, and in the proper amounts, would induce the color and the intensity desired — as well as all other craft skills associated with glassmaking. Even in the early days of the industry, the exceptional could be found in Pittsburgh's

Originally called "variegated glass," multi-colored creamers — these creamers made in the region between 1880 and 1900 are part of a large creamer collection donated to the Historical Society by a Pittsburgh woman — mimicked more expensive agate ware ceramic and marble pieces. By tinkering with glass formulas, manufacturers could issue inexpensive copies of luxury items.

glass. "Mr. Robertson ... had some very handsome specimens of purple glass," one visitor, Anne Royall, remarked in 1828, "and seems to vie with Bakewell & Co. in industry and skill in manufactory of white flint."[11]

Fine colorless glass also was often delicately engraved, and all clear and cut glass was prized for its reflective qualities during the period, for homes relied on candles or windows for light. The way a looking glass, mirror, or a chandelier with glass prisms could reflect, and thus increase, light helped to endear such items to their owners. Using Leighton's formula, however, high quality colorless glass could be made cheaply, opening a broad market for many products of the Pittsburgh region's glasshouses.

Within a few short years, home decorators were also demanding new styles and applications for colored glass, to be coordinated with other aspects of interior and home design. The association with fashion ensured that certain colors and designs would go out of style, to be replaced by new patterns and colors. Suddenly, chemistry became very important in the glasshouse, and by the 1870s, chemistry had also begun to greatly influence glass design. Anyone who possessed the necessary technical expertise, be they glasshouse owners such as Thomas Atterbury, professional "colorists" working in the factories, or eventually trained chemists, had a hand in how glass products looked. Formulas were often closely guarded secrets, known only to a few men at each company.

A new color of glass was worth a lot of money if popularly received, and, additionally, product lines with established consumer appeal also could be produced in a variety of colors. Adams & Company's popular Wildflower pattern, for example, was sold in colorless, amber, vaseline (yellow), blue, and apple green (as in Granny Smith apples). One mold produced five different sets of colored glass.

Other formulas developed during the period allowed glass designers to create objects that replicated ceramic materials. Milk glass, popularized by Atterbury & Co.'s "White House" factory on Pittsburgh's South Side, provided the cheaper alternative to high-end materials such as porcelain. The Atterburys turned out a plethora of this opaque white or colored (primarily blue and green) tableware and novelties in the 1870s and '80s. Several of the milk glass animals, made as containers for food products such as mustard, borrowed from 18th and 19th century tureens. Rabbits on ceramic tureens made as serving pieces for rabbit stew, and boar's heads on soup tureens of porcelain from English factories, as well as partridges, doves, and birds made as covered bowls or boxes, provided a precedent for glass designers to expand upon. Covered glass dishes in the form of owls recall the Parian ware owls also made in the 1870s. Some glassware was also made to mimic earthenware such as majolica, popular in the 19th century. Heads of cabbage, melons, basket-weave patterns, and leaf plates all appeared in both glass and ceramic. The popularity of naturalistic subjects in the late 19th century — bringing all of the outdoors, its flora and fauna, into the home — contributed to the appeal of such forms.

Milk glass also brought splashes of color into the home. The soft opaque blues mimicked the color of

The dramatic shading of the "Sunset" rose leaf jar (1924-1927) came from exposing the finished yellow-colored form to the heat of the furnace's "glory hole." The shading was inspired by more expensive ceramic and art glass colors.

Persian ceramic tiles, which enjoyed a revival in popularity in Europe from 1860s through the 1880s. Slag or mosaic glass made at several glasshouses — Atterbury & Co. in Pittsburgh, Challinor, Taylor & Co. in Tarentum, and Westmoreland Specialty Co. in Grapeville — recalled the agate used in jewelry or imported marbles. The blending of colors — purple, green, or caramel, each swirled with white — required an advanced understanding of glass chemistry.

Stains or enamel were media for decorating glass even less expensively. The ruby staining of pattern glass offered a popular alternative to expensive cased and cased cut glass. Cased glass is made from two or more glass layers of different colors gathered atop one another and then shaped. After annealing, the top layer could be cut back in a pattern to expose the layer underneath — a labor-intensive process requiring skill and experience. Decorating companies in Pittsburgh, such as the Oriental Glass Co., specialized in "ruby-staining," which created a similar effect at a fraction of the price. For a time, the company had a site at the Pittsburgh Exposition Building near the Point. Visitors could buy a piece of glass as a souvenir with their name and the date of their visit, or whatever else they desired, painted over or engraved in a ruby stain. Glass decorated by Oriental (most likely) and marked "Souvenir of the Pittsburgh Exposition" still turns up today.

One part of the modern glass industry where color remains an important

Introduced in 1927, Consolidated Lamp & Glass' bubbly green "Catalonian" line copied the "Old Spanish" and Mexican glass imported in the 1920s. Diamond Glass of Indiana, Pa., answered Catalonian with "Barcelona" (in pink, c. 1930).

design consideration is in tableware, for consumers and designers are known to coordinate their selections with other aspects of interior design or decoration. For instance, golds and greens dominated the decorator's palette of the 1970s for wall and accent paints, upholstery, and even household appliances. Household glass of the period used the same palette. An advertising brochure for Fayette Glass (a division of L.E. Smith Co. of Mt. Pleasant, Westmoreland County) shows vases, ashtrays, tableware, and accent pieces in amber and avocado green, and the Colonial Revival colors of blue and red that surged in popularity around the Bicentennial.

Modern glass companies continue to rely on color specialists to ensure that what they make is coordinated with trends in interior design.

By 1900, manufacturers increasingly relied on and employed individuals who specialized in both the design and development of new glass products. We have seen how, previously, responsibility for design had shifted from glassblowers, owners, and traveling agents to mold-makers and management. By the later years of the 1800s, while mold-makers still had input into design, companies also began to hire or contract with industrial designers, chemists, technicians, and engineers, to develop new products. Designers continued to draw upon the larger world of fine and decorative arts, current events and politics, and the natural world for inspiration. Glass manufacturers were also now responsive to science and the laboratory where experimentation with the physical properties of glass led to both the development of new products and new applications for glass products.

The career of designer Reuben Haley (1872-1933) bridged the great changes that swept through the glass industry in the late 19th and early 20th centuries. His father, English immigrant Jonathan Haley, spent much of his career as a mold maker and machinist in Pittsburgh's glass industry. Among the elder Haley's accomplishments were important innovations in the design of machine presses, which, as discussed earlier, were critical to the rise of Pittsburgh as a glass city. Between 1867 and 1873, he refined and patented a more durable pressing machine — it was also easier to operate — that could withstand the differential pressure exerted when the lever or plunger was engaged. By 1873, the year after his son Reuben's birth, the press was widely used in the industry. Eventually Jonathan Haley and another of his glassworker sons established a mold shop in Ravenna, Ohio.[12]

Reuben Haley, surrounded from birth by glass and metal workers, began his own career as a die maker for

Opposite page: A "pillar-molded" bar bottle (c. 1850, and most likely made in Pittsburgh) was designed to be both beautiful and sturdy. Below: McKee Glass' birdhouse (c. 1950) seemed like a good idea, but birds found it too hot to call home and it flopped on the market.

a Massachusetts silver company. He then switched to glass design for a number of concerns. Eventually he returned to the Pittsburgh region to work at factories in Ohio and Western Pennsylvania. Haley maintained a keen awareness of design trends, and applied them prolifically to glass. For example, he was among the leading designers of pressed glass imitations of cut glass that were popular at the turn of the century. His Chippendale line, produced at the Lancaster, Ohio, plant of the National Glass Co. trust, was inspired by Georgian influences of the day. In 1911, Haley became chief designer for the giant United States Glass Co. trust, where he rose to vice president, was active in the manufacturer's association, and took a leading role in the organization and running of the annual Pittsburgh trade show (see Chapter 4). That position gave him ongoing contact and familiarity with the consumer market for glass.

Above: Designer Reuben Haley's Katydid vase is a direct copy of French designer Rene Lalique's Sauterelles vase. Nude figures popular in art of the 1910s and '20s inspired Haley's Dancing Nymphs pattern (c. 1928).

Differences with new ownership caused Haley to resign from U.S. Glass in 1925 and move from Pittsburgh to Beaver County, where he continued to work independently for a number of glass companies. He is perhaps best known for work in this final period of his life, between 1925 and 1933. Haley's designs, executed for the Consolidated Lamp & Glass Co., demonstrated his understanding of modern art. Several of his pieces show the direct influence of French artist Rene Lalique. Haley's Katydid vase, introduced by Consolidated in 1926, interprets Lalique's style by borrowing directly from the Frenchman's "Sauterelles" vase of the early 1920s. The use of naturalistic motifs in heavy relief, flowers, animals, and insects draws on the tradition of Lalique and Art Deco practitioners. His rich blues and greens, as well as his use of crystals and opalescents, reveal Haley's awareness of French jewelry design and their visual and decorative arts.[13] Haley's glass design "named 'Martele' certainly is worthy of attention," urged an influential trade publication. "The new line is the closest made in this country to the production of Lalique, the well known French artificer in glass."[14]

Perhaps the best known and most appreciated of Haley's designs during the period is the Ruba Rombic glass pattern (by Consolidated) that he unveiled in January of 1928. The line of familiar tableware pieces, with its distinct angular motif, drew directly on Cubist visual art of the period. Influenced by fine art and by new designs in silver, Haley fully developed a design introduced by other glassmakers.[15] The marketing campaign for wholesalers and retailers borrowed language, terms, and graphic design directly from the Art Moderne movement. ("Ruba Rombic, An Epic in Modern Art,"read the public relations material.) Haley's tableware was certainly art, even taking on architectural effects: his glass cast shadows that transfigured light. Mysterious color names for the Ruba Rombic line heightened its appeal: "smoky topaz," "jungle green," and "honey," among others. Obviously both the glass and the marketing touched a chord, for just three months later, the Kopp Glass Co. in the Pittsburgh suburb of Swissvale introduced its Modernistic line. With Ruba Rombic, Haley demonstrated the influence of the industrial designer, not just in developing new molds for glass, but in controlling color and developing advertising that set the tone he chose for marketing the glass. Some industrial designers did more than design; they also helped devise the marketing strategies for making glass desirable to the public.

Sculptured art glass designed by Haley and made by Phoenix Glass in the 1930s used birds, fish, and flowers in naturalistic decorations. This is the Wild Geese pattern, c. 1933.

The career of "color man" Nicholas Kopp bridged the same period as Haley. Trained on the factory floor, he rose to a management position at Consolidated, then participated in founding a new factory in Swissvale. Like Consolidated, the company specialized in the production of lighting. But both Kopp and his glass company were best known for their manipulation of color and chemistry. With many design innovations in color to his credit (and an advertising campaign for "Kopp Kolors"), Nicholas Kopp is perhaps best known for developing the formula for selenium red glass. While its first applications were for tableware and lighting, its most long-lived use has been a technical one. Selenium red is prized because it reads as a true red when interacting with light, and the color holds true when projected over long distances. The enhancement in safety this red glass offered found wide application for railroad switches and signals. Kopp still uses the selenium formula in manufacturing glass for traffic signals used on roadways and railroads, at airports, in radio tower beacons, and in exterior lights for airplanes.

While men with sufficient technical and scientific knowledge to produce colored glass had worked in the industry since the middle decades of the 19th century, it was not until this century that professionals such as chemists and scientists worked in glass factories. Innovators like Nicholas Kopp had learned on the factory floor through constant experimentation and trial, but by 1910, college-educated professionals were also doing such work. The change coincided with the building of research and development facilities by the larger glass companies. James Chambers' research and development center at American Window Glass in Allegheny City (now Pittsburgh's North Side) was one of the first such facilities. John Lubbers and his team of engineers and mechanics developed the Lubbers machine process for flat glass at Chambers' site. Companies in the region such as Pittsburgh Plate Glass soon followed suit.

Another example is Macbeth-Evans, where one of the industry's first college-educated scientists, Alexander Silverman, began his career. After graduating from the University of Pittsburgh in 1902 with a bachelor of philosophy degree, Silverman spent two years in the laboratory at Macbeth-Evans' Charleroi plant, 35 miles southeast of Pittsburgh. Since he had no specific training in glass chemistry, he spent the bulk of his time experimenting with the raw materials. Key results were glass batch compositions that did not require constant testing and checking, which convinced Silverman of the chemist's importance in glass manufacturing. Themes he returned to often in his writing were the economy and product quality that a partnership of science and industry promised.

Silverman became an instrumental figure in glass research, and in the training of scientists in the industry, while spending much of his career in an academic setting. From his faculty appointment at Pitt in 1905 until his retirement in 1951, he also worked as a consultant to glass companies. He concentrated his research in three areas: theoretical considerations; industrial and commercial applications; and the chemical constituents of glass production. Silverman received over 20 patents for microscope illuminators and coloring agents for glass, and published over 200 articles and several longer works. His impact was broad and diverse, from quality control of the molten batch, to development of formulas and colors for use in table, container, and signal glassware, to advancing other sciences by refining optical glass, especially for microscopes (with applications in biology, astronomy, and the military). He also studied the reflective qualities of glass and its application to optical glass, mirrors, and photography.[16]

Silverman was a seminal figure as well for his encouragement of other scientists in the field, having begun his career at the time when glass companies first glimpsed the commercial benefits of applied science. Money invested in scientific R&D proved valuable in the development of new machinery and production processes, as well as in the standardizing of those processes that affected quality. (See Philip Scranton's excellent discussion of this point

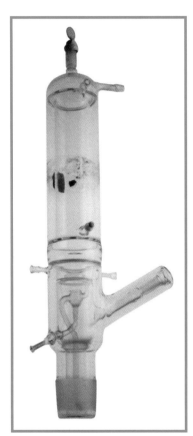

Scientists rely on glass in the laboratory, and glass companies now rely on scientists to drive research and development efforts. One of the industry's first trained scientists was Alexander Silverman, who began his career early this century at Macbeth-Evans' Charleroi, Pa., plant.

in his introduction.) The company laboratory became the site for innovation, and many glassmakers that survived changes in the industry and prospered did so because they invested in R&D. When Silverman began his career, he could list only six other glass chemists working in the American industry (Frederick Gelstharp at Pittsburgh Plate Glass, Robert Linton and Robert Frink at American Window Glass, George Barton at the Whitehall-Tatum Co., Henry Hess at the Libbey Glass, and Douglas Nash at Tiffany and Co.). By Silverman's retirement, a majority of large glass operations employed trained chemists.

An example of laboratory innovation with wide ranging applications was the development of heat tempered glass. By altering formulae with the addition of borisilicates, Corning Glass Co.'s development was able to withstand heat. The New York company's product, valued for its use as chemical glass and in industry, found popular application in glass oven ware marketed by Corning as Pyrex. The Fry Glass Co. of Rochester, Pennsylvania, signed a licensing agreement with Corning to produce and sell the glass as "Fry Oven Glass." Realizing the previously untapped potential for this product, the McKee Glass Co. of Jeannette produced a line they called "Glasbake."

All three companies had to find ways to make their revolutionary new product lines acceptable to consumers. Something we now take for granted — that glass can go in the oven — was practically unthinkable in 1915. The principal consumer was the homemaker. The media included recipe books with "educational" pages featuring home economists using glass oven ware, and advertisements in newspapers and magazines, such as *Ladies Home Journal*, similar to those seen in recipe books. The industry also mounted an aggressive campaign of live demonstrations. Once the consumer felt comfortable with the material, specialized lines of oven ware were introduced. Oven ware was decorated, sold with metal or chromium holders (so it could go from oven to table), and even produced for storing foods in the refrigerator (so that food could go from oven, to table, to refrigerator and back to the oven again, entirely in glass). By 1923, a trade journal recorded that

> Fry Oven Glass... is today one of the most highly appreciated cooking and baking utensils to be found in the modern home. This line of ware... consists at the present time of something over 100 items including casseroles, bread bakers, pie plates, pudding dishes, meat platters, cake plates, utility trays, biscuit trays, tea pots, coffee percolators,

Understanding the chemistry of color in glassmaking led to new effects in lighting, such as the soft blue glow of the 1870 "marriage lamp."

roasters, custard cups, etc. The slogan selected by the Fry Company for their oven line is "A Dish For Every Use."[17]

In 1922, Fry introduced perhaps the most innovative use for its oven glass, from a similar formula named "FOVAL" (Fry Oven Art Line). This art glass, made in a multitude of forms including lamps, vases, compotes, and candlesticks, extended the reach of oven ware far beyond the kitchen. A new glass, created in the laboratory and made palatable to the public for everyday use, had been recast for sale in high-end decorative lines.[18]

Research and development went on, of course, in other branches of the industry, too. By 1927, Pittsburgh Plate Glass employed 31 men at its research lab north of Pittsburgh in Creighton, where research on plate, window, optical, and structural glass went on. The company's research innovations, in tandem with marketing and product development, were critical to successful introductions of new products.

The success of structural glass, for example, evolved greatly during the first part of the 20th century. In 1907, Pittsburgh Plate Glass introduced "Carrara" glass. Its smooth, shiny surface, available only in white, looked like marble. At first, Carrara was marketed as an alternative to marble — not a cheaper alternative, but a more sanitary one. But during a boom of large public building construction that soon ensued, Carrara proved to be an ideal material for spaces such as public restrooms, where its nonporous qualities remedied sanitation concerns. It could sheath walls where germs might lurk.

Pittsburgh Plate Glass sold Carrara for use not only in restrooms, but also for dentist's offices, operating rooms, and even morgues. An illustration in the company's 1923 *Yearbook* compared marble and Carrara under magnification to reveal that marble actually has a porous surface.

The late 1920s marked the evolution of Carrara, also available by then in black, for decorative and functional uses in all public areas, indoor and outdoor. Its colors and sophisticated, sleek ethic were perfect for modern — and modernizing — sensibilities. Marketing appeals were aimed at small business owners, encouraging them to renovate their business with stylistic integrations of structural glass, aluminum, and brushed metals; Pittsburgh Plate Glass ads showed photographs of storefronts, restaurants, and business interiors before and after renovation. The company sent an exhibit of miniature storefronts around the country in

The glass lid made by H.C. Fry Glass of Rochester, Pa., (c. 1930) withstood the heat of popping corn and allowed the cook to see the kernels.

its "Modernize Main Street" campaign. Advertisements in *Architectural Digest* and other trade publications sold Carrara as the material to make the old new again.

Scientists, engineers, and technicians today still explore new uses or applications for glass. For instance, the design of glass windshields is closely coordinated with automobile design and technology. Modern windshields not only offer protection and visibility but have a variety of high-tech duties in today's autos. Some have reflective coatings that block out sun, enhacing pas-senger comfort while improving the efficiency of car air-conditioners. PPG Industries' Sungate Antenna Windshield has a built-in radio antenna. Other antennae in the product line allow electronic mapping or tracking of the vehicle, cellular phone functions, and transmit signals to a range of receivers, such as garage door openers and toll collection devices. In addition, the "Sungate" windshield's color can be coordinated with vehicle color and design. Commerce involving the automobile accounts for roughly one-quarter of America's economic activity, and, as we have seen throughout the history of glass, consumer demand and the profits to be gained from meeting that demand provide a powerful fuel for the human imagination.[19]

A company's industrial designers, scientists, and salesmen combine talents to make the laboratory's discoveries acceptable and understandable to con-sumers. Merely designing or inventing something new is never enough, for ultimately, advancements in consumer products must also sell, if true success is to be claimed. Converting fashion and function alike into sales requires the integration of knowledge with culture.

The symbolic nature of glass — its "meanings" in society — have changed over time, and manufacturing glass objects relevant to contemporary life requires an understanding of those changes. Pittsburgh Plate Glass real-ized in the early years of the 20th century, when the American public was concerned with sanitation, clean water, pure food, and germ-free environ-ments, that its innovative Carrara glass fit the bill as an attractive, nonporous, easy-to-clean material with a variety of useful applications. Similarly, manufac-turers of glass bottles and containers recognized the transparent nature of glass was a valuable selling point, so slogans such as, "Buy it in glass, see what you buy," were born. One constant in glass salesmanship for consumer food products has been the "clear advantage" of glass over alternative pack-ing materials such as ceramics or metal.

When "modernization" emerged in the mid-1920s as a cultural force — an idea intricately associated with advances in hygiene and other fields of sci-ence earlier in the century — PPG reinvented Carrara, introducing new colors

An advertisement in House and Garden, *December 1935, trumpets the remodeling potential of "Carrara" glass, made by Pittsburgh Plate Glass. Such campaigns signaled the beginning of the era when large companies that traditionally had served industrial customers targeted homeowners and other "end-use" consumers.*

and packaging it as an expression of progressive design for architects and building contractors. To recall another example, several glassmakers traded on similar impulses when introducing and updating the image of glass oven ware and tableware during these periods.

What held true in the first half of the 20th century — that understanding cultural and historical events and trends was instrumental in the design and marketing of glass — is still true today. The oil embargo of the early 1970s (and the first Earth Day) helped to focus the attention of the American public on the environment. Many manufacturers, including those that make architectural glass and glass containers, began to revise their marketing strategies to address environmental concerns. Industry-wide recycling campaigns and PPG's reflective glass are prime examples. Glass with reflective coatings found wide application not only in the automotive industry, but also in architecture and in the construction industry. Controlling heat and light transmission in all types of structures reduces energy consumption dramatically. Likewise, melting recycled glass to make new glass saves energy. Industry trade and interest groups such as the Glass Packaging Institute are prominent national advocates for glass as an environmentally friendly packaging material.

The institute in 1994 conducted focus group research which indicates the buying public shares certain of the institute's positions. Glass is said to have "product integrity": food or beverages packed in glass are "perceived to be

Above: Studies show that consumers perceived foods packaged in glass as pure or sanitary, so a 1996 poster by a glass manufacturers' trade group capitalized on that perception. Right: The hotel and restaurant trade snapped up the intuitively designed glass "hottle" (hot water bottle) when it came on the market in the 1940s.

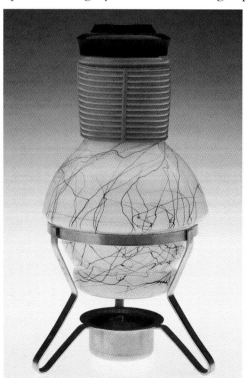

clean/sanitary, fresh, pure, truer tasting, natural, honest and reflective of the good old fashioned, traditional values of a bygone era."[20]

Three characteristics of glass packaging — its transparency, the ease with which it is made tamper resistant, and its reusability — appear to constitute the public's perception of product integrity. Glass also has a quality image. In fact, quality is a claim for the Pittsburgh region's glass that James O'Hara used nearly two centuries ago to sell his products. Meanwhile, documenting the public's desire for recyclable containers has important implication for the design of many kinds of consumer products. Cultural relevance serves the entire glass industry well by affecting, in subtle but constant ways, the choices made every instant in a consumer society.

In form and an explosion of color, the designer of this bowl (Duncan Miller Glass, Washington, Pa., c. 1930) celebrates the wide-open pattern of the chrysanthemum flower.

Today

Today there are some 20 factories and a half-dozen glass artist's studios in the region. Whether turning out 1 million square-feet of float glass a day, as PPG Industries' Meadville plant does, or creating objects of art such as Kathleen Mulcahy's 1998 "Golden Spinner Group" (right), glass remains a marriage of elemental ingredients, searing heat, and human hands. Opposite page: This publication's companion exhibition, which opened in April 1998 at the Senator John Heinz Pittsburgh Regional History Center, traces the area's glass history from its start to the present time.

The story of glass in Western Pennsylvania presents both continuity and change; an undulating, wavy ribbon from the region's glasshouse furnaces, 200 years long and now longer, weaves together past and present, places and people: glasshouse owners Gallatin and O'Hara; craftsmen Eberhart, Reitz, and Reppert; mold-makers and machinists Marshall and Beck; salesmen Pears, Ranney, and Sailer; technical innovators Arbogast, Leighton, and Owens; scientists and designers Silverman, Haley, and Kopp — and these are but a fraction of those whose names flare in the molten flow and will not fade in the history of Pittsburgh glass.

Old stories; families remember — a grandfather, a son, my aunt worked there and there and also there. Always the glass reminds us. So fragile, yet a reflection that shatters notions about Pittsburgh; glass, the Iron and Steel City's first industry and always as important as the steel industry. Through glass, we see clearly the region's past. New chapters in the story are being written as well. One such chapter was begun on a cold November day in 1995 in an open field along U.S. 119 south of New Stanton in Westmoreland County. With a thrust of a shovel into the hard earth, ground was broken for a new glass factory. Sixteen months later, one of the plant's two gas-fired furnaces

American Video Glass near New Stanton in Westmoreland County is part of the new wave in Western Pennsylvania glass-making. The company builds glass components at its giant complex for Sony. The company's diverse workforce includes many women working on the production line as well as in the offices. Opposite page: The glass TV components can weigh 100 pounds, so robots do the repetitive, physical, and dangerous work once done by laborers.

was lit — unwittingly on the bicentennial anniversary of the first glasshouse's firing in the region. There is little about the mammoth American Video Glass Co. plant that James O'Hara or Albert Gallatin would recognize. Its scale is immense: 750,000 square-feet of floor space. Unlike at Gallatin or O'Hara's site, no river meanders past the factory door; instead a rail spur juts out to the rear of the factory, and over the near hill interstate traffic thunders. No pile of coal restrains the factory's spread. Indeed, it sprawls across a hundred acres. A few hundred yards away stands another mammoth structure, a manufactory with a short, unusual name not part of the region's glass story: Sony.

American Video Glass, just across the road from Sony, builds glass components for Sony's television tube factory. About 500 American Video workers, using robotic arms and computer-driven controls, turn out products on a scale that O'Hara and Gallatin could not contemplate. The volume of raw materials staggers the mind. Two furnaces melt up to 675 *tons* of material a day to create some 4 million units of finished glass a year. Like the James O'Hara-Isaac Craig union of 1797, American Video is a joint venture — not of men, but of corporations: Sony Electronics and Corning Asahi Glass, Ltd. (That latter is itself a partnership, of Corning, Inc., of New York and the U.S.

subsidiary of Asahi Glass Co. of Japan.) The combination joins international wealth and experience in a $300 million start-up.

Just as it was to O'Hara and Craig, recruiting and retaining workers is important to American Video Glass. Turn-of-the-19th century businessmen were wholly dependent on their workers and they sought to employ sober and industrious men with the knowledge to build the furnaces, manipulate the formulas, and fashion the glass. For a while, their skills  drove the industry. By contrast, workers at American Video Glass were chosen not for their work experience or skills in glass manufacturing, but for many other factors, including personal characteristics and psychological traits. Each applicant faced a screening process intended to produce what company President Donald Dicken called "a highly flexible, empowered workforce capable of self-management."[1]

Being hired at American Video Glass takes an average of 30 to 45 days. Phone interviews generally begin the process. Then comes role-playing exercises in which the applicant is observed in a series of one-on-one and group situations. A 300-question personality test rounds out the day of role-playing. One worker described the exercise as "the hardest thing I ever did. You have no idea how you're doing or what they think. I went home and said to my wife, 'That's it. I don't think I made it.' Later they called and said I passed."[2] If applicants impress at both exercises, they begin a series of interviews and evaluations, reference checks, and other more traditional application procedures.

The screening process is part of a management system used in only about 5 percent of America's factories. The "skill-based career development program" fits the culture and environment at both Sony and American Video Glass. On-the-job training to develop individual technical skills and teamwork lasts for five years. And the rigorous hiring process helps to identify people inclined to succeed, thus making it more likely that the company's $5 million investment in recruitment and training is rewarded. The management structure is relatively "flat," with the goal being a high-performance work system run by self-directed or self-managed teams.[3]

Employees tested equipment, quality control programs, and training procedures for seven months. A little less than two years after groundbreaking, the plant was officially dedicated in October 1997 and began to move toward full production.

Across Western Pennsylvania can be found other glass manufacturers that have weathered the changes in the industry over the last 100 years. As the

For location of towns and factories in this chapter, see maps on page 158.

Many products once made of glass are either obsolete or are made from different materials. The U.S. Fish and Game Service used glass specie jars made by H.C. Fry Glass in Rochester, Pa., (c. 1925) for stocking streams with fish hatchlings. Right: Once dominated by glass factories employing thousands of people, Jeannette (here, c.1915) is today home to just two hot glass factories and only about 100 people take home a glass company paycheck.

geographical core of glassmaking, as well as production technology, marketing, and design have evolved, so too has the organization and management of the glass business. The industry faced a long series of challenges in the 20th century, including enormous alterations in U.S. political, social, and cultural life, as well as competition from national and international producers and from alternative materials. Some changes rendered some glass products obsolete. For instance, the widespread application of electricity made lamp chimneys largely unnecessary. Once produced by the tens of millions, by the 1930s the world's largest producer, Western Pennsylvania-based MacBeth-Evans, cast about for new markets for its product. Sales persisted in rural areas of the South and in countries such as Cuba, but the market gradually declined. In 1936, the company changed hands. It ceased to be family-owned and became part of Corning Glass. Production at the company's plant in Charleroi, still in business today, gradually shifted to tableware and eventually to Pyrex ovenware. As this book goes to print, the factory's future is in question. To focus on technical lines such as liquid crystal display glass, fiber optics, and high-purity fused silica for integrated circuits, Corning sold its housewares division, which included the Charleroi plant, to a New York investment company.

Other events reorganized and restructured the industry. Passage in 1918 of the 18th Amendment, which prohibited the sale of alcohol, was a serious blow to glass container manufacturers. During 15 years of Prohibition, bottle production for beer, wine, and distilled spirits plummeted, as well as affecting producers who specialized in bar ware. The Depression further thinned the number of regional glassmakers. "Two things saved us in the 1930s," recalls

View of Glass Factories, Jeannette, Pa.

Paul Sailer, retired head of sales and marketing for McKee Glass Co. "We produced those giveaways for movie theaters and soap boxes and we owned real estate in Jeannette. Every week before we paid the workers, we took their rent out of their pay. Those houses kept the company going during the Depression."[4]

At the same time the industry battled external economic forces, the marketplace grew increasingly competitive. Indeed, alternative materials played a significant role in the regional and national decline of the glass industry. In the early 20th century, for example, glass trade journals sounded the alarm on the danger of paper cups. The flint glass unions went so far in 1917 as to urge a boycott of soda fountains that served ice cream and drinks in paper cups. They argued that paper hurt their "trade, by reducing work for tumbler shops...."[5] The *National Glass Budget* opposed boycotting of "helpless business men, whose only alternative is to keep step with freak legislation, submit to fines or go to jail," and recommended the glass industry focus its ire on state legislators.[6]

Plastics posed an even more serious threat. By the 1940s, synthetics had broken through for consumer and domestic use, as well as in industry. *Architectural Record* in July 1940 detailed the industrial potential of plastics, especially in architecture. In contrast to materials such as glass,

> The entire history of building has been one of adaptation of "natural" materials to man's specific structural needs. Only recently has he been able to "pre-design" materials with new properties or new combinations of old ones. The huge and complex family of synthetic plastics is a striking illustration of this new-found ability to arrange a few molecules in an almost limitless number of combinations, each with widely varying forms, properties, etc. Already the plastics have attained extraordinary significance in building design; and they promise more for the future.[7]

The language of marketing plastics was remarkably similar to that used for glass. Plastics were "lightweight, flexible, moldable, homogeneous, 'bend' light, etc."[8] Unlike glass, however, they were "non-shatterable." The high cost and severe shortage of plastics in the World War II era were determining factors in its widespread application. The federal government recognized the problem, and helped to spearhead laboratory work with plastics. Even before the research was applied to production, *Architectural Record* boldly stated about plastic: "We cannot draw an accurate diagram of the future of plastics in architecture. Of one thing we can be sure: that future will be great and all-embracing."[9]

Aluminum was another serious challenger to glass. After technical advances in the 1880s had made large-scale aluminum production affordable,

PPG's float glass line in Meadville, rendered by local painter Cynthia Cooley (c. 1990) turns out enough glass for 20,000 automobile windshields every day.

the material steadily began to displace steel in many applications. For many years in the early 20th century, aluminum was a compliment to glass in architecture. But experimentation and further efficiencies in production brought aluminum's price down to a point that aluminum competed with glass as a packaging material for consumer goods. Most beverage cans in the United States were made of tin-plated steel as late as the 1950s — with glass monopolizing the bottle and container market — but early in the 1960s, Pittsburgh-based Alcoa began trials of steel cans with aluminum ends that incorporated a pull-tab opener. Consumers did not need a special "church key" for opening such cans. Alcoa aggressively marketed the "easy open" aluminum top — the company even sponsored a professional golf tournament that played off the tab-top name — and by 1963 had captured 40 percent of the canned beer market; within five years, market-share topped 80 percent and Alcoa had

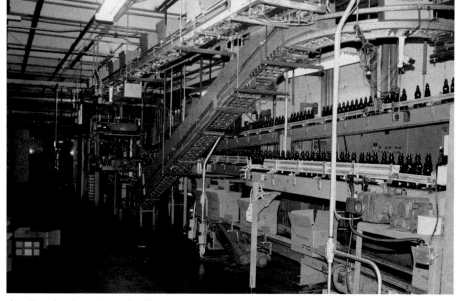

A million bottles a day roll off the conveyor lines of Glenshaw Glass, just north of Pittsburgh. Among its customers in 1998 was Mrs. Butterworth's.

aimed its sights at non-alcoholic beverages.[10]

Upstarts made progress on other fronts, as well. Formica, Marlite, and ceramic challenged Cararra glass for dominance in the kitchen and bath. The synthetics, especially, came in a plethora of colors and surface textures and were inexpensive, lightweight, easy to install and, like glass, sold as sanitary.

As aluminum and plastics became major players, and production costs in the fully mature American glass industry continued to rise, glass also had to contend with competition from cheaper imports. The technology of glassmaking, once standardized, allowed new industries to thrive wherever raw materials, fuel, and labor were plentiful. Mexican tableware entered the American market as early as the 1920s. Asian countries were competing by the 1970s.

Plants in Western Pennsylvania began to close in the late 1960s. The last remaining factory of the once mighty U.S. Glass trust in Tiffin, Ohio, closed in 1968. The McKee Glass Co., in business for almost 150 years, changed hands several times and was finally shuttered in the 1980s. Westmoreland Glass, just a few miles away in Grapeville, soon followed. Throughout Ohio and West Virginia, other giants of the tableware industry closed — Fostoria, Imperial, and Cambridge among them. Battles over wages and a long strike contributed to the demise of most window glass factories in the region. Cheap labor abroad and south of the U.S. border placed pressure on American glass makers to keep costs competitive. And, it must be said, many companies were simply unable or unwilling to make the capital investments to modernize operations that could keep them competitive in the global marketplace of the late 20th century.

Part II

Glass industry survivors in the region have found a variety of ways to compete. Some identified a niche market and focused their operations to service it, while others took an opposite approach, stripping out unprofitable parts of their glass operations while diversifying into allied industries.

Kopp Glass, L.E. Smith, and Youghiogheny Glass have succeeded to different degrees using the first strategy. Kopp, which began as a lamp and lighting producer, now thrives with traffic signals, aircraft lighting, and airport taxiway lights. The Swissvale company turns out 90 percent of all aviation shade glass in the world, safely guiding pilots into airports around the globe. With over 1,200 molds in stock, the company survives and thrives by filling small, specialty orders. Larger glass manufacturers have the technology to produce such products, but their factories require large orders to run cost-effectively. As Bruce Stephens, Kopp's head of manufacturing, explained, "We thrive on the 50 and 100 piece order."[11]

New frontiers offer new opportunities. Kopp Glass of Swissvale is a leading international producer of runway markers and aircraft lighting.

L.E. Smith, which primarily makes giftware, survives through close ties to clients that go back decades, while Youghiogheny is one of the few American companies to manufacture opalescent window glass. Using an efficient casting method, the firm makes small batches of glass in colors and textures prized in the manufacture of stained glass lampshades and related items.

Glenshaw Glass, in the suburb north of Pittsburgh for which the company is named, adapted the niche strategy to a larger scale. "A big bottle company might run Pepsi molds for six months of the year," explained company machinist Norm Patton. "We found our niche by developing a highly trained group of machinists who can change the molds on the automated machines every four hours if needed. We do the short runs that no one else wants to

Inaugural gifts for presidents Reagan, Bush, and Bill Clinton, below, were all made by glass companies in the Pittsburgh area. Artist Steve Fenstermacher blows the bowls (top and below) at Youghiogheny Art Glass in Connellsville, then master cutter Peter O'Rourke engraves them at Lenox in Mount Pleasant.

do."[12] Family-run for 90 years, Glenshaw grew into a huge international conglomerate in just over a decade after the first non-family member joined the board in 1986. Interloper John Ghaznavi went on to buy the company in 1988 and to completely change its direction. Applying skills gained outside the glass business, he modernized the plant, rebuilding one furnace and increasing output capacity by one-third. He also invested liberally in the latest technology, reached agreements with company unions, and built a management team with experience in glass. In 1993, his parent company, G&G Investments, acquired a controlling interest in the troubled Canadian container producer, Consumer Packaging. In 1996, Glenshaw again expanded, purchasing a half-interest in Anchor Glass from the Mexican container company Vitro. In 1988, Glenshaw was a $33 million company; by 1997, the conglomerate, with plants in Western Pennsylvania and Canada as well as Ukraine, Italy, and Israel, was valued at $1.6 billion. (A development occurring as this book was being readied for publication was Glenshaw's takeover of the former Anchor bottle plant in Connellsville, Fayette County, where, among other items, Rolling Rock beer bottles are made.)

Another glassmaker still operating in Western Pennsylvania is Lenox Co. The New Jersey-based firm, known best as a china company, added glass to its product line in the late 1960s by purchasing the Bryce Brothers factory in Mount Pleasant, Westmoreland County. Lenox then

built a new facility in Mount Pleasant, complete with a factory showroom and offices. Lenox's fine handmade stemware, sold largely in jewelry stores and finer department stores, is the American rival to Irish Waterford Crystal and its marketing is directed at wedding and special occasion sales. The glass line allows Lenox to market a coordinated table setting of china, glass, and flatware.

PPG Industries, meanwhile, took a different path, expanding through acquisition and internationalization, partnering with competitors, and diversifying its product base. In 1968, Pittsburgh Plate Glass changed its corporate name to signal that it was more than a glass company. With multiple businesses — glass, coatings, and chemicals — PPG Industries is better able to weather downturns in single sectors of the marketplace. In addition, coordination across business units allows the company to develop new products in a holistic way; for instance, tinted automotive glass color-coordinated with automotive paint, which it also manufactures.

PPG has pursued joint ventures with a number of competitors, to share expenses and to expand into new markets. Joint ventures have resulted in partial ownership of fiberglass factories in Venezuela and Taiwan, and a facility for custom cutting of basic flat glass and specialty glasses in Japan. One PPG float glass plant still operates in Western Pennsylvania, in Meadville, 80 miles north of Pittsburgh. (PPG also owns fiberglass factories in England and The Netherlands.) No fiberglass is made in the region, though R&D facilities for both continuous strand (fiber) glass and flat glass are in the area. Automotive windshields are made at Creighton, site of the company's first factory, about 10 miles north of Pittsburgh on the Allegheny River. Pittsburgh remains the corporation's home, but its glass production takes place around the country and around the world.

For several decades, regional glassmakers have served international as well as domestic customers. Among the foreign brands that Glenshaw Glass made bottles for between 1950 and 1965, for example, were Rica (Guatemala) and, far right, Cuba's Santa Teresa.

Most glassmakers in Western Pennsylvania have been companies and corporations turning out consumer and industrial products. However, a few glass artists have always worked in the region. One such operation is Pennsylvania Art Glass, in Burrell Township near Pittsburgh, owned by Ed Nesteruk and Ed Kachurik. The uncle-nephew team concentrate on "veiled" glass, in which glass sprayed with coloring agents is covered with additional glass layers to create distinctive, abstract imbedded designs. Their objects are sold in gift stores and art galleries across the country.

Other contemporary glass artists in the Pittsburgh area include Kathleen Mulcahy and Ron Desmett. They are partnering with the community of

Elizabeth, south of Pittsburgh on the Monongahela River, to build a school and studio for glass study and artistic production — the Elizabeth Glass Workshop — drawing on the rich cultural heritage associated with glass in towns along the river.

Examining glass and the 200-year history of the industry in Western Pennsylvania provides an excellent case study for understanding industrial development in the region and the nation. From two small factories, the region grew to dominate the national market and to wield influence interna-

Industrial Hot Glass Producers of Western Pennsylvania

Bridgeville	*GE Lighting, Bridgeville Glass Plant*
Brockway	*Owens-Brockway Glass Containers*
Charleroi	*Kohlberg, Kravits, Roberts & Co.*
Connellsville	*Youghiogheny Opalescent Glass Co., Inc.*
	Anchor Glass Container Co.
Creighton	*PPG Industries*
Crenshaw	*Owens-Brockway Glass Containers*
Floreffe	*Guardian Industries Corp.*
Glenshaw	*Glenshaw Glass Co., Inc.*
Jeannette	*Jeannette Specialty Glass*
	St. George Crystal, Ltd.
Latrobe	*GBC Material Corp.*
Meadville	*PPG Industries*
Monaca	*Phoenix Glass Plant, Anchor Hocking Specialty Glass Co.*
Mt. Pleasant	*Smith Glass Co.*
	Lenox Co.
	American Video Glass Co.
Pittsburgh	*Plum Glass Co.*
Port Allegany	*Ball-Foster Glass Container Co.*
	Pittsburgh Corning Corp.
Punxsutawney	*Raymond Dereume Glass, Inc.*
State College	*Corning Asahi Video Products Co.*
Swissvale	*Kopp Glass, Inc.*
Tipton	*PPG Industries*
Wellsboro	*OSRAM Sylvania*

tionally. Glass made in Western Pennsylvania has travelled the oceans, been
to the moon, and provided views across innumerable landscapes.

Whether inspired by fine art or born in the laboratory, the glass transformed from sand to substance by fiery heat and imbued with meaning by
the hands of those who made, sold, and saved it, is central to Western
Pennsylvania's heritage. Glassmaking was integral to Pittsburgh's position as
America's industrial powerhouse, and promises to continue its influence on
the region's future.

*In 1976, TRACO of Pittsburgh,
using glass made by PPG
Industries, installed its replace-
ment windows in New York's
Statue of Liberty. As noted at
the beginning of the book,
Pittsburgh glass is all around us.*

APPENDIX I

Citations

Complete citations for the numerous standard city directories, widely available in libraries, are not provided.

CHAPTER 1

[1] Samuel Johnson, in *The Rambler*, — this publication is an English newspaper published 1750-1753; exact date of essay unknown — as quoted in Chloe Zerwick, *The Short History of Glass* (Harry N. Ambrams, Inc., 1990), 13.

[2] George Wallis, *The Art Journal, The Illustrated Catalogue of the Universal Exhibition* (Virtue, 1868).

[3] "Pittsburgh's Leading Industries," *Pennsylvania Historical Review*, 1886, 84.

[4] *American Pottery & Glassware Reporter*, May 13, 1880 (indexed in the J. Stanley Brothers Files, Corning Museum Library, Corning, N.Y.).

[5] *National Glass Budget*, Jan. 15, 1921, 2.

[6] Used often as a column insert in *National Glass Budget*; also used in a similar form, "Purity. Glass says it. Glass sells it.," by the Glass Packaging Institute in its publications, c. 1996.

[7] *National Glass Budget,* March 9, 1901, 1.

CHAPTER 2

[1] Stephen Ambrose, *Undaunted Courage* (Simon & Schuster, 1996), 94.

[2] Thomas Ashe, *Travels in America Performed in 1806* (R. Phillips, 1809), 19.

[3] Ibid., 19.

[4] Raymond Walters, Jr., *Albert Gallatin: Jeffersonian Financier and Diplomat* (Univ. of Pittsburgh Press, 1969), 133-43.

[5] Albert Gallatin Letters, Sept. 6, 1795, Gallatin Papers, New York Historical Society. (Hereafter "GP, NYHS")

[6] Gallatin to J.W. Nicholson, Nov. 24, 1797, GP, NYHS.

[7] Gallatin to J.W. Nicholson, March 9, 1798, GP, NYHS.

[8] In addition to the Gallatin Papers, several biographies exist on this subject, including the one sited. For an excellent and detailed account of the early years of the Gallatin factory, see also Ken Wilson and Helen McKearin, *American Bottles and Flasks and Their Ancestry* (Crown Publishers, 1978).

[9] Craig Papers, July 18, 1800, Carnegie Library, Pittsburgh.

[10] James O'Hara Papers, June 1810, Historical Society of Western Pennsylvania Archives. (Hereafter "OP, HSWP")

[11] Information gleaned from detailed reading of Pittsburgh city directories.

[12] Hogg Family Papers, Historical Society of Western Pennsylvania.

[13] Pittsburgh City Deeds, Nov. 17, 1832, Allegheny County Recorder of Deeds, Pittsburgh.

[14] 1850 Federal Population Census and 1860 Federal Population Census, National Archives, Washington, D.C.

[15] OP, HSWP, July 1805. Frieze (Philip R. I. Friese) was an investor in and proprietor of the Baltimore glassworks of Frederick Magnus Amelung at the time he wrote O'Hara.

[16] OP, HSWP, Nov. 21, 1806.

[17] OP, HSWP, reports.

[18] OP, HSWP, Letterbook, April 19, 1811.

[19] OP, HSWP, Letterbook, Dec. 4, 1809.

[20] OP, HSWP, 1812-13, Production Report.

[21] OP, HSWP, Letterbook, Oct. 28, 1809. General information about the distribution of products comes from a complete reading of the Letterbook.

[22] OP, HSWP, Letterbook, July 5, 1811.

[23] James Leander Bishop, *History of American Manufacturers,* volume 2 (Edward Young & Co., 1864), 156.

[24] Christina H. Nelson, "The Pittsburgh Glasshouse of Bakewell and Ensell: A Contemporary Description," *Glass Club Bulletin* 137 (1982), 10-13.

[25] *St. Louis Gazette*, April 1809 (page number unavailable).

[26] Thomas Nuttal, *A Journey of Travels into the Arkansas Territory During the Year 1819*, vol. XII, 45 (Univ. of Oklahoma Press, 1980), 45.

[27] *Warren County Messenger*, July 30, 1829.

[28] All quotes from James Bryce's journals, transcript and copy, HSWP Archives, Pittsburgh.

[29] Copy of indenture reproduced in Lowell Innes, *Pittsburgh Glass 1797-1891: A History and Guide for Collectors* (Houghton, Mifflin, 1976), 37.

[30] Bryce Journal, HSWP Archives.

31 Benjamin Page letter to John Hammond, HSWP Archives, Jan. 3, 1825.

32 See Catherine Reiser, *Pittsburgh's Commercial Development 1800-1850* (Penna. Historical and Museum Commission, 1951), for a complete discussion of state transportation systems.

33 I am indebted to Arlene Palmer Schwind for providing transcribed copies of the 1820 U.S. Census of Manufactures.

34 Page letter to John Hammond, Jan. 3, 1825, HSWP Archives.

35 Ibid.

36 Bishop, 250.

37 Joseph M. Rogers, *The True Henry Clay* (Philadelphia: Lippincott Co., 1904)., 218.

38 Page letter to John Hammond, Jan. 3, 1825, HSWP Archives.

39 1826 Pittsburgh city directory, 69.

Chapter 3

1 Elizur Wright letter to Susan Clark, Library of Congress Manuscripts Division, Nov. 24, 1828, quoted in, "The Black City: Elizur Wright Jr.'s View of Early Industrial Pittsburgh," *Western Pennsylvania Historical Magazine* 55:3, 250.

2 Kenneth M. Wilson and Kirk J. Nelson, "The Role of Glass Knobs in Glassmaking and Furniture," *Antiques*, May 1996, 753.

3 Ibid., and Kirk J. Nelson, "Progress Under Pressure: The Mechanization of the American Flint Glass Industry, 1820-1840," master's thesis, Univ. of Delaware, 1988, 111-125.

4 Quoted in Nelson, "Progress Under Pressure," 116, from *Journal of the Franklin Institute* 3 (April 1829), 258.

5 Nelson, "Progress Under Pressure," 3.

6 This is attested to by a letter in the Archives of the Wheaton Village Museum of American Glass, Millville, N.J. Mold maker Monroe Husted documents his time in creating three molds for McKee, ranging from 87.5 to 378 hours.

7 Helen McKearin and Kenneth Wilson, *American Bottles and Flasks and Their Ancestry,* 411.

8 Information compiled from Bishop, Pittsburgh city directories and the Dun Records, Baker Library, Harvard Univ.

9 *Pennsylvania Historical Review*, "Washington Beck entry," (Historical Publishing Co., 1886), 60.

10 "Minute Book of the Macbeth-Evans Glass Co.," HSWP Archives, Evans Family Papers, Feb. 10, 1910.

11 Information based on unpublished research conducted by undergraduate intern Edward Slavishak for HSWP in city directories and period reviews of industry.

12 Pittsburgh city directories 1860-75; *Pittsburgh Press*, "Old Time Glass Blower Sighs as Plant is Razed," Aug. 23, 1931.

13 Dennis Zembala, "Machines in the Glasshouse: The Transformation of Work in the Glass Industry, 1820-1915," doctoral dissertation, George Washington Univ.,

1984), 192.

14 Ibid., 201.

15 Ibid., 203.

16 Ibid., 194.

17 Joseph Weeks, *Report on the Manufacture of Glass* (David Williams, 1883), 1048-1050.

18 Historic American Buildings Survey, "Town of Jeannette" (unpublished report; HABS No. PA-6087), 5.

19 *Greensburg Evening Press*, "A Glass City to be Built at Grapeville," (Jan. 1888; exact date unknown), 1.

20 HABS, 6-8.

21 Numbers based on research conducted for HSWP in the Dun Records, Baker Library, Harvard Univ., by Arlene Palmer Schwind; research in city directories and the *Crockery and Glass Journal* 1902 trade directory by Gary Pollock, Lauren Uhl, and the author.

22 Beaver County city directory, 1908.

23 Weeks, 1050.

24 Weeks, 17.

25 *The Diary of Elbridge Gerry, Jr.* (Brentano's, 1927), 107.

26 Weeks, 6-7.

27 Elizabeth Beardsley Butler, *Wage Earning Pittsburgh* (Survey Associates, 1914), 282.

28 *Saturday Evening Post,* Nov. 17, 1906.

29 John W. Larner, "The Glass House Boys," *Western Pennsylvania Historical Magazine* 48:4, 362-363.

30 Letter from Central Glass Works, HSWP Archives, no date.

31 Ibid.

32 Weeks, 1043-1045.

33 Zembala, 336-339.

34 Ibid., 339.

35 Macbeth-Evans Minute Book, Nov. 17, 1909, Evans Collection, HSWP Archives.

36 Zembala, 341-342.

37 Zembala, 342.

38 Larner, "The Glass House Boys," 355.

39 Zembala, 344-345.

40 Richard John O'Connor, "Cinderheads and Iron Lungs: Window-Glass Craftsmen and the Transformation of Workers' Control, 1880-1905," Ph.D. dissertation, Univ. of Pittsburgh, 1991, 31. This work is an excellent source for understanding the changes in work and workers' lives as automated technology was introduced.

41 Marg Iwen, "Michael J. Owens: The Man and His Machines," in *Glass Collectors Digest*, April-May 1996, 80-82.

42 Weeks, 1048.

43 C.J. Phillips, *Glass The Miracle Maker* (Pitman Publishing, 1941), 206-209.

44 *China, Glass & Lamps* advertisements, Feb. 1931, 9, and Aug. 1930, 7.

45 *China, Glass & Lamps*, Feb. 20, 1928, 14.

Chapter 4

1 James O'Hara Papers, Letter to James Morrisson, June 24, 1805, Historical Society of Western Pennsylvania Archives. (Hereafter "OP, HSWP")

2 OP, HSWP, Letterbook, March 12, 1805.

3 OP, HSWP, Letterbook, 8.

4 Ibid.

5 Ibid., July 29, 1811.

6 *Pittsburgh Gazette*, May 18, 1838.

7 William Lyford, *The Western Address Directory* (J. Robinson, 1837).

8 Thaw Family Papers, HSWP Archives, John Thaw Expense Book, May 2, 1818.

9 Pittsburgh city directory, 1841; thanks to Kyle Husfloen, who shared with me the advertisement from the *Northwestern Gazette and Galena Advertiser*, Galena, Ill., Feb. 20, 1836.

10 Tom Pears Letters, Private Collection, Oct. 18, 1818.

11 Ibid., Jan. 5, 1820.

12 Ibid., July 29, 1820.

13 Ibid., May, 1820.

14 Ibid., June 2, 1820.

15 Ibid., June 25, 1820.

16 *China, Glass & Lamps*, Nov. 6, 1922, 16.

17 *Pottery, Brass & Glass Salesman*, Dec. 16, 1920 — reprinted in James Measell, *New Martinsville Glass, 1900-1994* (Antique Publication, 1994).

18 *National Glass Budget*, Jan. 14, 1899, 2.

19 Ibid.

20 *China, Glass & Lamps*, Nov. 6, 1922, 12.

21 Ibid., Jan. 7 and Feb. 3, 1917.

22 *National Glass Budget*, Jan. 24, 1914, 3.

23 Ibid., Jan. 17, 1920, 1.

24 *China, Glass & Lamps*, Jan. 28, 1924, 1.

25 *National Glass Budget*, Jan. 7, 1922, 8.

26 Ibid., Jan. 21, 1922, 3.

27 Fredonia Jane Ringo, *China and Glassware* (A.W. Shaw Co., 1925), vi.

28 Ibid., ix.

29 *National Glass Budget*, May 23, 1936.

30 *Fifty Years of Glass Making 1869-1919* (Macbeth-Evans Glass Co., 1920), 35-36.

31 *National Glass Budget*, May 23, 1936.

32 *China, Glass & Lamps*, Sept. 1936, 8.

CHAPTER 5

1 James O'Hara Papers, Letterbook, Nov. or Dec. 1809, HSWP Archives, Pittsburgh.

2 Elias Fordham, *Personal Narrative of Travel* (Arthur H. Clarke Co., 1906), 75, 76.

3 Anne Royall, *Mrs. Royall's Pennsylvania or Travels Continued in the United States* (published by author, 1829), vol. 2, 124.

4 A letter from Tom Pears to his wife Sarah dated Sept. 10, 1816, and held in a private collection, establishes that Jardelle had been in Pittsburgh at least since that year.

5 Jane Shadel Spillman, *White House Glassware: Two Centuries of Presidential Entertaining* (White House Historical Association, 1989), 26-35.

6 *Farmer's Register* (Greensburg, Pa.), May 2, 1801, as quoted in *Made in Western Pennsylvania* (Historical Society of W. Pa., 1982), 10.

7 *The Illustrated Family Christian Almanac,* 18.

8 Colleen McDannell, *Material Christianity* (Yale Univ. Press, 1995), 57.

9 Based on research using a Rudy Brothers list of commissions, c. 1903, and Pittsburgh city directories from the period.

10 *National Glass Budget*, Jan. 20, 1917, 15.

11 Royall, 125.

12 Dennis Zembala, "Machines in the Glasshouse," 278-85.

13 For an excellent presentation of the life and work of Reuben Haley, see Jack D. Wilson, *Phoenix & Consolidated Art Glass 1926-1980* (Antique Publications, 1989); for more on the work of Lalique, see Patricia Bayer and Mark Waller, *The Art of Rene Lalique* (Wellfleet Press, 1988).

14 *National Glass Budget*, Jan. 16, 1926, quoted in Wilson, 16.

15 *China, Glass & Lamps*, May 9, 1927, 18, carried an ad for Westmoreland Glass Co.'s 101 line. The item featured, an ice bucket, that was designed with angular lines to resemble a large chunk of ice.

16 Unpublished research by Carnegie Mellon Univ. undergraduate intern Edward Slavishak for HSWP; Silverman's biography in *The National Cyclopedia of American Biography* (J.T. White, 1930), and a reading of his publications in chemistry, ceramics, and glass journals.

17 *National Glass Budget*, Jan. 20, 1923, 1.

18 Discussion draws upon information in trade journals and magazines such as *China, Glass & Lamps*, *Ladies Home Journal* advertisements, and *The Collectors Encyclopedia of Fry Glassware* (Collectors Books, 1990).

19 PPG Automotive Products "cut-sheet," Nov. 1994, on Sungate Antenna Windshield, 4076E.

20 Glenn Bauer & Associates, Inc., "Consumer Attitudes Regarding Glass Packaging," prepared for Glass Packaging Institute, Oct. 1994, 8-10.

CHAPTER 6

1 *Pittsburgh Post Gazette*, June 12, 1997.

2 Interview with American Video Glass worker Joe Scott, Sept. 3, 1997.

3 This discussion is based both on newspaper coverage of the plant opening in the *Pittsburgh Post Gazette* in Oct. 1997, and an interview conducted with Mike Wolf of American Video Glass, Sept. 16, 1997.

4 Interview with Paul Sailer, April 1993.

5 *National Glass Budget*, Feb. 3, 1917, 5.

6 Ibid.

7 *Architectural Record*, July 1940, 66.

8 Ibid., 68.

9 Ibid., 76.

10 George David Smith, *From Monopoly to Competition: The Transformation of Alcoa, 1888-1986* (Cambridge Univ. Press, 1988), 339-342.

11 *Pittsburgh Post Gazette*, March 21, 1996, E-1.

12 Interview with Norm Patton, July 1996.

Image Descriptions and Credits

COVER

TOP, LEFT

"Ruba Rombic" liquor bottle, six whiskeys, and tray, c. 1930, Consolidated Lamp & Glass Co., Coraopolis, Pa.; "Jungle Green" glass, pressed, and blown molded.
Museum Purchase, Hillman Foundation Funds; Matt Bulvony Photography

TOP, CENTER

Grouping of glass pieces from the collections of the Historical Society of Western Pennsylvania.
Matt Bulvony Photography

TOP, RIGHT

Compote or sweetmeat, c. 1860, Bakewell, Pears & Co., Pittsburgh; colorless lead glass, pressed in the "Argus" pattern.
Museum Collection; Matt Bulvony Photography

BELOW

Washing and drying after acid etching, H. C. Fry Glass Co., Rochester, Pa., c. 1910
Courtesy of Robert Batto

BACK COVER

Bowl, c. 1930, Duncan Miller Glass Co., Washington, Pa., cobalt glass, pressed.
Museum Purchase, Tri-State Depression Era Glass Society Funds and Hillman Foundation Funds; Matt Bulvony Photography

INSIDE FRONT COVER

Feeding the furnaces, Creighton Pittsburgh Plate Glass factory, c. 1920
Courtesy of PPG Industries, Inc.

PAGE X

Airport, traffic and railroad signals, c. 1995, Kopp Glass, Inc., Swissvale, Pa., red and yellow glass, pressed.
Gifts of Kathleen J. Hansen, Kopp Glass, Inc., and Dean Six; Matt Bulvony Photography

CHAPTER 1

PAGE 1, BACKGROUND

U.S. Glass Co., Glassport, Pa., c. 1950
Courtesy of Cora Ott

INSET

Interior of McKee Glass Co., Jeannette, Pa., c. 1905
Gift of William Kindelan

PAGE 2

Rose colored goblet, H.C. Fry Glass Co., Rochester, Pa.; blown with pattern molding, c. 1925
Gift of Anne Madarasz; Matt Bulvony Photography

PAGE 3, TOP

Jar, 1800-40, attributed to New Geneva Glass Works, New Geneva, Pa.; aqua green glass, blown.
Jug, 1800-45, attributed to New Geneva Glass Works, New Geneva, Pa.; blown in a pattern mold with 24 vertical ribs.
Tumbler or jelly glass, c. 1800, probably Monongahela Valley; blown in pattern mold with 24 ribs.
All are gifts of Mr. and Mrs. J. Harry Gorley; Matt Bulvony Photography

PAGE 3, BELOW

Press Shop, South Side, Pittsburgh, c. 1910
Gift of Al Bierman

PAGE 4

Three "Loop" pattern lamps, 1865-95, James B. Lyon & Co., Pittsburgh; colorless glass, pressed.
Gift of T. Reed Ferguson; Matt Bulvony Photography

PAGE 5, TOP

Glass ball, c. 1880, probably Agnew & Co., Pittsburgh, for Captain Bogardus; amber glass, blown molded.
Gift of Merton J. Deyo; Matt Bulvony Photography

PAGE 5, RIGHT

Letter from James O'Hara to Joseph Carson, June 20, 1810
Gift of Mrs. Harmar Denny

PAGE 5, BELOW
Model "T" Ford, *Courtesy Frick Art & Historical Center Car and Carriage Museum, Pittsburgh.*
Collection of G. Whitney Snyder;
Photograph by Lynn Snyder

PAGE 5, BELOW, INSET
Headlight lens, c. 1918, Macbeth-Evans Glass Co., Pittsburgh; colorless glass, pressed.
Gift of Laura Ford and Emory Moran Ford;
Matt Bulvony Photography

PAGE 6, TOP
PPG Place
Courtesy of PPG Industries, Inc.
PAGE 6, BELOW
Ship crossing the Miraflores Locks, Panama Canal, 1995
Courtesy of Panama Canal Commission

PAGE 7
Postcard of Fort Pitt Glass Works, c. 1910
Gift of Irene and Paul G. Sailer

PAGE 8, TOP
"Carrying the Finished Plate," Pittsburgh Plate Glass Co. catalog, 1901
Gift of Frances A. Taylor

PAGE 8, BELOW
Decanter and stopper, c. 1830, Stourbridge Flint Glass Works, Pittsburgh; colorless lead glass, blown with cut decoration.
Gift of Mrs. John B. Sellers on behalf of Mrs. Thomas A. Mellon and Mary and Elizabeth Wightman;
Matt Bulvony Photography

PAGE 9
Goblet, c. 1910, acid-etched decoration by Joseph Locke, Mt. Oliver, Pa.; cobalt over colorless glass with platinum leaf decoration.
Museum Collection; Chisholm Photographic

PAGE 10, TOP LEFT
Glass chain, c. 1920, made by Albert C. Meyer at Glenshaw Glass Co., Glenshaw, Pa.; colorless glass, handmade.
Gift of Henrietta Meyer Garrett; Matt Bulvony Photography

PAGE 10, TOP RIGHT
Oil lamp, c. 1905, Consolidated Lamp & Glass Co., Coraopolis, Pa.; opaque white glass and metal, hand-painted decoration, pressed.
Museum Purchase, Hillman Foundation Funds;
Photographed by Chisholm Photographic

PAGE 10, BELOW
Catalog, *National Glass Co., Pittsburg, Pa., Export Catalogue No. 2,* 1904
Gift of Paul G. Sailer

PAGE 11
Glass slippers, c. 1900, U.S. Glass Co., Pittsburgh; blue glass and green glass, pressed.
Bequest of Mrs. Harry G. Dunmire;
Matt Bulvony Photography

PAGE 12
"Oval Sett" creamer, c. 1880, Challinor Taylor & Co. or U.S. Glass Co., Pittsburgh; white glass with hand-painted decoration, pressed.
"Ribbed Palm" creamer, c. 1865, McKee Brothers, Pittsburgh; colorless glass, pressed with applied handle.
"Cornell" creamer, c. 1898, Tarentum Glass Co., Tarentum, Pa.; colorless glass with gold painted trim, pressed.
"Swag Block" creamer, c. 1895, George Duncan & Sons and U.S. Glass Co., Pittsburgh; colorless glass with ruby stain, pressed.
"Daisy and Button with Crossbar" creamer, c. 1890, Richards & Hartley, Tarentum, Pa.; blue glass, pressed.
"Fleur-de-lis and Tassel" creamer, c. 1891, Adams Glass Co., Ripley & Co., and U.S. Glass Co., Pittsburgh; green glass, pressed.
All are bequest of Mrs. Harry G. Dunmire;
Matt Bulvony Photography

PAGE 14
Covered bowl or "sweetmeat," c. 1835, Midwest; colorless lead glass, pressed in "Midwestern hairpin" pattern.
Museum Purchase, Hillman Foundation Funds;
Matt Bulvony Photography

CHAPTER 2
PAGE 15, BACKGROUND
Early blown goblet, 1800-20, possibly New Geneva Glass Works, New Geneva, Pa.; green glass, blown in a pattern mold with 16 ribs.
Gift of Mrs. Alan S. Davison; Chisholm Photographic

PAGE 15, INSET
"The Glass Furnace II," reprint of Diderot engraving, Vol. X, Verrerei en Bois, Pl. IV
Gift of Irene and Paul G. Sailer

PAGE 16
Early blown goblet, 1800-20, possibly New Geneva Glass Works, New Geneva, Pa.; green glass, blown in a pattern mold with 16 ribs.
Gift of Mrs. Alan S. Davison; Chisholm Photographic

PAGE 34, TOP
"Map of the National Road between Cumberland and Wheeling"
Courtesy of the Illinois State Historical Library

PAGE 34, BELOW
Henry Clay, by Frederick and William Langenheim, 1850, from *Encyclopedia Brittanica*, vol. 4, page 698; Helen Hemmingway Benton, Publisher, Chicago, 1974.
Library & Archives Collection

PAGE 35, TOP
From *Davy Crockett's Almanack's1835- 1843, The Nashville Imprints*, reprint ed., Pioneer Press, Union City, Tenn.
Used by permission.

PAGE 35, BELOW
Cruet with stopper, c. 1830, possibly Pittsburgh; blue glass, blown in a pattern mold with 16 ribs swirled left.
Museum Purchase, Browne Fund;
Matt Bulvony Photography

PAGE 36
Shop jar with cover, 1840-75, possibly Pittsburgh; colorless glass, blown.
Museum Purchase, Hillman Foundation Fund
Shop jar, 1840-75, probably Bakewell, Pears & Co., Pittsburgh; colorless lead glass, blown.
Gift of Mr. and Mrs. R. V. Nuttall
Covered jar, 1830-80, possibly Bakewell, Pears & Co., Pittsburgh; colorless and blue glass, blown.
Gift of Janet and John Clever in memory of Ednah Knox Swigart; Chisholm Photographic

PAGE 38
Compote, c. 1845, Mulvany & Ledlie, Pittsburgh; amethyst over colorless lead glass, blown and cut with 16 panels.
Gift of Mrs. Lida Hogg Snowden Henesey;
Chisholm Photographic

CHAPTER 3
PAGE 39, BACKGROUND
Vase, c. 1910
Pittsburgh Lamp Brass, & Glass Co., Swissvale, Pa.; white glass with hand-painted decoration, blown.
Museum Purchase, Hillman Foundation Funds;
Chisholm Photographic

PAGE 39, INSET
Engraving, Cunningham & Ihmsen Glass Works, Galaxy Publishing Co., Philadelphia, c. 1870
Library & Archives Collection

PAGE 40
Vase, c. 1910, Pittsburgh Lamp, Brass, & Glass Co., Swissvale, Pa.; white glass with hand-painted decoration, blown.
Museum Purchase, Hillman Foundation Funds;
Chisholm Photographic

PAGE 41, TOP
Bakewell window pane, 1835-45, Bakewell, Pears & Co., Pittsburgh; colorless lead glass, pressed.
Museum Purchase; Matt Bulvony Photography

PAGE 41, BELOW
Compotes and cup plate, c. 1835, Fort Pitt Glass Works, Pittsburgh; colorless lead glass, pressed and blown.
Museum Purchase, Pittsburgh Chapter, National American Glass Club Funds; Chisholm Photographic

PAGE 42, TOP
Cowboard, c. 1930, McKee Glass Co., Jeannette, Pa.; wood, glass and metal.
Gift of Paul G. Sailer; Chisholm Photographic

PAGE 42, BELOW
Swan Lamp, c. 1870, Atterbury & Co., Pittsburgh; colorless and blue glass, pressed.
Star paneled lamp, c. 1885, Co-operative Flint Glass Co., Beaver Falls, Pa.; blue glass, pressed.
Lamp, c. 1885
King Glass Co., Pittsburgh; blue green and opalescent glass, blown molded and pressed.
Lamp, c. 1875
Atterbury & Co., Pittsburgh; colorless and blue opalescent glass, pressed.
Gift of Janet and John Clever in memory of Ednah Knox Swigart; Matt Bulvony Photography

PAGE 43
L.E. Smith press, date unknown
Gift of L. E. Smith Co.; photographed by Jenn Smith, HSWP

PAGE 44, TOP
Paddle and tongs, c. 1975, used at Westmoreland Glass Co., Grapeville, Pa.; metal, wood and asbestos.
Museum Purchase; Chisholm Photographic
Page 44, below
"Pittsburgh Sketches — Among the Glass Workers," from *Frank Leslie's Illustrated Weekly*, March 18, 1871
Library & Archives Collection

PAGE 45
Patent No. 236,140, W. Beck, "Mold for the Manufacture of Hollow Blown Ornamented Glassware," Jan. 4, 1881
Courtesy of the U.S. Patent and Trademark Office

PAGE 99, TOP
Candlesticks, c. 1870, Ripley & Co., Pittsburgh; opaque and translucent gray glass and metal, pressed.
Museum Purchase, Hillman Foundation Funds; Chisholm Photographic

PAGE 99, BELOW
Crucifix lamps, c. 1920, U.S. Glass Co., Factory K, Pittsburgh; frosted colorless glass, pressed.
Gift of Helen Gallagher Southworth; Matt Bulvony Photography

PAGE 101
Watercolor study for stained glass window, c. 1925, possibly J. Horace Rudy for Rudy Bros. Co., Pittsburgh; graphite, ink, and watercolor on board.
Gift of Mrs. Charles Rudy

PAGE 102, TOP
J. Horace Rudy, artist for Rudy Brothers Studio, c. 1900
Gift of the Estate of Mrs. Charles Rudy

PAGE 102, BELOW
Compote, c. 1880, Crystal Glass Co., Pittsburgh; colorless glass, pressed.
Gift of Joyce J. Johnston; Matt Bulvony Photography

PAGE 103
Frog covered dish, c. 1890, probably Atterbury & Co., Pittsburgh; white and green glass, pressed.
Duck covered dish, c. 1885, Atterbury & Co., Pittsburgh; white and blue glass, pressed.
Owl covered dish, c. 1890, probably Pittsburgh; white glass, pressed.
Gifts as memorial to Sarah Jane Atterbury McGinley, and Museum Collection; Chisholm Photographic

PAGE 104
Creamer, c. 1890, probably Atterbury & Co., Pittsburgh; green slag glass, pressed.
"Flying Swan" creamer, c. 1890, Westmoreland Glass Co., carmel and white slag glass, pressed.
"Oval Sett" creamer, c. 1880, Challinor, Taylor, Tarentum, Pa.; purple and white opaque slag glass, pressed.
Bequest of Mrs. Harry G. Dunmire and gift of Frances A. Taylor; Chisholm Photographic

PAGE 105
"Sunset" rose leaf jar, 1924-27, Co-operative Flint Glass Co., Beaver Falls, Pa.; yellow to red glass, pressed.
Gift of Roy D. and Adam M. S. Ash; Matt Bulvony Photography

PAGE 106
"Catalonian" vase, c. 1930, Consolidated Lamp & Glass Co., Coraopolis, Pa.; green glass, blown.
Museum Purchase, Hillman Foundation Funds
"Barcelona" vase, c. 1930, Diamond Glass Co., Indiana, Pa.; pink glass, blown molded.
Museum Purchase, Rainbow Diamond Depression Era Glass Club Funds; Matt Bulvony Photography

PAGE 107
Bar bottle, c. 1850, possibly Pittsburgh; colorless lead glass with blue threading, blown molded.
Museum Purchase, Brendel Fund; Matt Bulvony Photography

PAGE 108
Birdhouse, c. 1950, McKee Glass Co., Jeannette, Pa.; opaque white glass with painted decoration and metal ring and bottom, pressed.
Museum Purchase, Hillman Foundation Funds; Chisholm Photographic

PAGE 109, TOP
"Katydid" vase, c. 1930, designed by Reuben Haley for Consolildated Lamp & Glass Co., Coraoplolis, Pa.; opaque white glass with painted decoration, pressed.
Gift of Scott Montroy and David Cleveland; Chisholm Photographic

PAGE 109, BELOW
"Dancing Nymphs" palace platter, c. 1928, Consolidated Lamp & Glass Co., Coraopolis, Pa.; colorless glass with applied amethyst ceramic color, pressed.
Museum Purchase, Hillman Foundation Funds; Matt Bulvony Photography

PAGE 110
Vase, c. 1933, Phoenix Glass Co., Monaca, Pa.; colorless glass with pale yellow wash and metal ormolu, pressed in the "Wild Geese" pattern.
Museum Purchase, Hillman Foundation Funds; Chisholm Photographic

PAGE 111
Laboratory glass , c. 1970, Gulf Research & Development, Harmarville, Pa.; colorless glass, blown.
Gift of William C. King; Matt Bulvony Photography

PAGE 112
"Marriage" lamp, c. 1870, Ripley & Co., Pittsburgh; opaque blue, translucent gray, and opaque white glass, and metal, pressed.
Bequest from the estate of Lowell Innes, gift of Mr. and Mrs. J. Bruce McWilliams; Matt Bulvony Photography

PAGE 113
Popcorn popper, c. 1925, Bersted Mfg. Co., Chicago, Ill., glass lid by H.C. Fry Glass Co., metal and opalescent glass, pressed.
Museum Purchase, Hillman Foundation Funds; Chisholm Photographic

PAGE 114
Advertisement, "Making Yesterday's Bathrooms fit for Tomorrow," from *House and Garden*, December, 1935
Courtesy of Hunt Library, Carnegie Mellon University

PAGE 115, TOP
"Glass Says It, Glass Sells It" poster, 1996
Gift of the Glass Packaging Institute

PAGE 115, BELOW
Hottle, c. 1940, McKee Glass Co., Jeannette, Pa.; white and black glass, plastic, and metal, pressed.
Gift of Gregory Smith; Matt Bulvony Photography

PAGE 116
Bowl, c. 1930, Duncan Miller Glass Co., Washington, Pa., cobalt glass, pressed.
Museum Purchase, Tri-State Depression Era Glass Society Funds and Hillman Foundation Funds; Matt Bulvony Photography

CHAPTER 6
PAGE 117, BACKGROUND
Detail of Golden Spinner group, 1998, Kathleen Mulcahy, assisted by Ron Desmett, Oakdale, Pa.
Museum Purchase, Hillman Foundation Funds and gift of Kathleen Mulcahy; Matt Bulvony Photography

PAGE 117, INSET
Photograph of *Glass: Shattering Notions* exhibit at the Senator John Heinz Pittsburgh Regional History Center, 1998
Photographed by David Kennedy

PAGE 118
Golden spinner group, 1998, made by Kathleen Mulcahy, assisted by Ron Desmett, Oakdale, Pa.
Museum Purchase, Hillman Foundation Funds and gift of Kathleen Mulcahy; Matt Bulvony Photography

PAGE 119, TOP
Aerial view of American Video Glass Co., Mt. Pleasant, Pa., c. 1997
Courtesy of American Video Glass Co.

PAGE 119, BELOW
American Video Glass Co. employees, c. 1997
Courtesy of American Video Glass Co.; Nakles Photography

PAGE 120
American Video Glass Co., Mt. Pleasant, Pa., 1997
Courtesy American Video Glass Co.

PAGE 121, TOP
Specie jars, c. 1925, H.C. Fry Glass Co., Rochester, Pa.; colorless glass, blown.
Gift of Dr. Clifton Dietz; Chisholm Photographic

PAGE 121, BELOW
Postcard, "View of Glass Factories, Jeannette, Pa.," c. 1920
Gift of Irene and Paul G. Sailer

PAGE 122
"Glass Making," by Cynthia F. Cooley, c. 1990, oil on canvas.
Courtesy of Cynthia F. Cooley

PAGE 123
Interior, Glenshaw Glass Co., 1998
Photograph by Tracy Walther

PAGE 124
Pittsburgh International Airport runway, c. 1985
Courtesy of Kopp Glass, Inc.

PAGE 125, TOP
Presidential bowl, 1996, made by Youghiogheny Glass and engraved by Lenox; colorless lead glass, blown with engraved decoration.
Courtesy of Lenox

PAGE 125, BELOW
Presentation of inaugural gift to President Bill Clinton, 1996
Courtesy of Lenox

PAGE 126
Soda and mineral water bottles, c. 1965, Glenshaw Glass Co., Glenshaw, Pa.; colorless and green glass with fired-on paint labels, machine made.
Gift of Henrietta Meyer Garrett; Matt Bulvony Photography

PAGE 128
Early morning view from the crown of the Statue of Liberty, New York, 1987
Courtesy of Matt Bulvony Photography; copyright Matt Bulvony Photograpyy

Profiles of Selected Western Pennsylvania Glass Companies from the 19th and 20th Centuries

Part of the preparation for both this catalogue and the exhibition, "Glass: Shattering Notions," involved unraveling the convoluted and interwoven histories of many glass companies in the region. A portion of that research is presented in the following company profiles, which are arranged alphabetically.

The text for each entry draws on primary sources in Pittsburgh, deed records, city directories, trade journals, and company advertisements, and also on research done for the Historical Society by Arlene Palmer Schwind in the Dun Records at Harvard University's Baker Library. In a few instances, information came from books on individual companies, regions, or segments of the industry.

Questions remain about many of the companies and their histories, and collecting information was difficult. Partnerships and corporations frequently changed principals and directors. Investors came and went. Factories burned or were moved. This is an attempt to present what could be learned, from the most readily available sources, about important glasshouses in the region and about some of the major companies still in business. It should not be considered an exhaustive chronicle of factory or company histories, but for those primarily interested in collecting Pittsburgh glass, we believe the information, gathered in one place for the first time, should prove valuable.

Many staff members of the Historical Society helped me finish collecting the dates and facts presented here, and a few of those same people also wrote some entries. Everyone who helped is noted in my acknowledgements at the front of the book.
*— **Anne Madarasz***

ADAMS & CO.

1851–1860	Adams, Macklin & Co., Ross and Second streets
1860—1891	Adams & Company, South 10th and Washington (now Sarah) streets
1891	Joined U.S. Glass Co. as Factory A

An accounting ledger indicates that John Adams, like many glassmen of the time, learned his craft at the esteemed Bakewell, Pears and Co. He worked for the firm as a presser in 1846. In 1851, Adams, Macklin & Co. opened on the corner of Ross and Second streets in the former Stourbridge Flint Glass Works. Their works was known by the nickname "Jenny Lind." In the early 1850s, Adams experimented with substituting lime for lead in glass production.

In 1860 or 1861, the firm moved to Birmingham, now Pittsburgh's South Side, and opened a factory at South 10th and Washington (now Sarah) streets. Principals during the late 19th century included John, Adolphus A., and William Adams, George F. Easton, Gottfried Miller, David E. Carle, and Samuel G. Vogeley. Several other names appear on deeds to additional South Side lots that Adams and Co. purchased, including William and Joseph Doyle, Ralph Johnston, Peter Kountzler, and John Malone. Joseph Doyle and John Malone are listed in contemporary city directories as glassblowers.

Adams & Co. produced lamp chimneys, fruit jars, and tableware. Among the firm's most popular pressed glass patterns are those known to collectors as Wildflower (originally Adams #140), Baltimore Pear, Moon and Star, and Thousand Eye.

Adams & Co. was among the Pittsburgh manufacturers at the Centennial Exhibition. Several of its items featured Centennial themes. Three lamps bore the inscription "1776–1876." An oval bread plate featured a Liberty Bell surrounded by the names of the signers of the Declaration of Independence. In honor of the celebration, Adams also produced tableware with the Liberty Bell which proved very popular.

AGNEW & CO.

c.1841–1847	Chambers & Agnew
1853	Blackford & Agnew
1854–1858	John Agnew & Co.
1866–1867	Agnew Son & Co.
1868–1871	Agnews & Wilcox
1871–1875	Agnew & Son
1876–1894?	Agnew & Co.

John Agnew was born in Beaver County in 1819. Three years later, his family moved to Pittsburgh. At age 14, he was apprenticed to glass manufacturer William McCully. He remained there five years, leaving in 1837. Agnew joined with Alexander Chambers in 1841 or 1842 to form Chambers & Agnew, a partnership which lasted five years. Their factory was on Carson Street (now 20th), below Penn Avenue in Pittsburgh. Agnew also married a Chambers (Mary Ann).

An ad in the 1847 Pittsburgh city directory indicates that Chambers & Agnew produced vials, bottles, window glass, and glassware in addition to "a Superior Article of Imitation Crown Window Glass...."

Like many glassmen, Agnew apparently formed a number of partnerships. References are scanty and confusing. However, Dun records, city directories, and other sources link his name in business with a Mr. Blackford, Lemuel Wilcox, and his son J. C. Agnew.

In the 1869–70 Pittsburgh city directory, Agnews & Wilcox advertised as manufacturers of vials, bottles, and green glassware. In 1880, the *Pottery & Glassware Reporter* noted that Agnew & Brown was producing 8-10,000 amber glass target balls per day. Although the firm does not appear in Pittsburgh city directories after 1894, Lowell Innes in *Pittsburgh Glass* mentions that an Agnew & Co. of Hulton (now Oakmont, an eastern suburb of Pittsburgh) was offering Shoo-fly flasks in that same year.

AMERICAN VIDEO GLASS CO.

June 1995	Company founded
Nov. 1995	Ground broken for new plant
Aug. 1997	Production begins

This newest of Western Pennsylvania glass factories, between Mt. Pleasant and New Stanton in Westmoreland County, is a 50-50 partnership between Sony and Corning Asahi Video Products, itself a joint venture between Corning Inc. and the U.S. subsidiary of Asahi Glass Co. of Japan. Located in a 700,000-square-foot facility across the street from a Sony television plant, the company currently produces the front panels and funnels for 27-inch and 32-inch televisions. At publication, these parts were being shipped to San Diego for assembly into televisions, but the potential exists at the Westmoreland complex to one day go from raw materials to finished television set.

ATTERBURY & CO.

1860–1861	Hale, Atterbury & Co.
1861–1864	Atterbury, Reddick & Co.
1864–1893	Atterbury & Co.
1893–1903?	Atterbury Glass Co.

Brothers James Seaman Atterbury and Thomas Bakewell Atterbury followed in the family footsteps by establishing themselves in the glass industry and taking active rolls in commercial and civic affairs in Pittsburgh. Their grandmother Sarah was a sister of Benjamin Bakewell, founder of the renowned Bakewell's glass company.

James and Thomas Atterbury joined brother-in-law James Hale to form Hale & Atterbury in 1860. (Some sources indicate 1858 or 1859.) Their White House factory was located on Carson Street at McKee Street (now 10th Street) on the city's South Side. Within two years, Hale was replaced by James Reddick, listed in contemporary city directories as a glassblower. Reddick left the firm in 1864, and the two brothers continued to manage the factory until passing it on to their sons in 1893. The operation moved to Carson and First streets in 1879.

In addition to managing the company, James served as president of the Cresson, Clearfield County and New York Short Line Railroad and Director of the Mechanics National Bank. Thomas was president of the Iron and Glass Bank. They also were elected to the Pittsburgh City Council and Birmingham Borough Council.

Atterbury and Co. made a variety of items including tableware, bar bottles, covered dishes, and lamps. Well-known among Atterbury's covered dishes are the opal or milk glass animal designs. These include a rabbit, duck, chick and eggs, bull's head, and boar's head. The firm was an industry leader in the manufacture of lamps, with annual lamp sales approaching 180,000. Atterbury won an award at the Centennial exhibition in 1876 for its lamps, chimneys, and globes.

Thomas Atterbury was particularly inventive and the Atterbury name appears on at least 110 patents (71 for inventions and 39 for designs). In 1865, the company received a patent for pressed glassware which incorporated a figure on the bottom that could be painted to resemble a cameo. Three years later, Atterbury patented a design for a screw socket to connect the base and font of kerosene lamps.

Atterbury was one of the companies that resisted the industry mergers of the 1890s. It remained an independent factory into the early 20th century. The company last appeared in the Pittsburgh city directory for 1902-03.

BAKEWELL, PEARS & CO.

1808–1809	Bakewell & Ensell
1809–1813	Benj. Bakewell & Co.
1813–1827	Bakewell, Page & Bakewell
1827–1832	Bakewell, Page & Bakewells
1832–1836	Bakewells & Anderson
1836–1842	Bakewells & Co.
1842–1844	Bakewell & Pears
1844–1880	Bakewell, Pears & Co.
1880–1882	Bakewell, Pears Co., Ltd.

This firm is perhaps the best-known of all the Pittsburgh glass companies. Founded by Englishman Benjamin Bakewell, the company was managed by a variety of partners in its history. The most long-lived associations included members of the Bakewell and Pears families, with important contributions from Benjamin Page in the early years. Though best known for the quality of its lead or "flint" glass and its fine cut and engraved glass, billheads and advertisements document the production of window glass, bottles, lamps, chemical ware, and apothecary shop furniture. The firm's reputation was enhanced by its

gift of two cut glass decanters to President Madison in 1816 and the subsequent purchase of cut tableware for the White House by Presidents Monroe and Jackson. The Bakewells also presented two cut glass vases to Lafayette when he visited Pittsburgh in 1825. A letter from Lafeyette, now in the Archives of the Historical Society of Western Pennsylvania, expresses his thanks for the gift.

The company factory, located near downtown at the corner of Water and Grant streets, appears in an early watercolor of Pittsburgh painted in 1817 by Emma Gibson. Many of the firm's skilled workmen were recruited in Europe and the cutting and engraving done by the firm shows the influence of these English and French craftsmen. The firm also recruited locally and became a great training ground for the second generation of Pittsburgh glasshouse owners, with men such as James Bryce and Thomas Evans beginning their careers there. One of the earliest companies to patent the pressing process, the company became adept at producing fine pressed wares. Both pressed furniture knobs and a window pane exist with the Bakewell mark.

Both the factory and the warehouse were lost, at a cost of $75,000, in the Great Fire of 1845. The company rebuilt at the same site, remaining until 1854, when it moved the factory across the Monongahela River to Bingham Street, between Eighth and Ninth streets, on what is now Pittsburgh's South Side. The firm operated until 1882, when the factory site was sold to Oliver Bros., a wire manufacturer. A c. 1875 catalog provides a record of the later wares of the company: blown urns and jars, fish bowls, lanterns, smoke bells, and pressed glass in patterns such as Argus, Thistle, Prism, Rochelle, Icicle, and Saxon. As late as 1876, when the company exhibited at the Centennial, it was still doing cut glass, evidenced by its large medal-winning bowl now in the collection of New York's Corning Museum.

BRYCE BROTHERS

1850–1854	Bryce, McKee & Co.
1854–1865	Bryce, Richards and Co.
1865–1882	Bryce, Walker & Co.
1882–1891	Bryce Brothers
1891	Joined U.S. Glass Co. as Factory B
1893–1896	Reorganized as Bryce Brothers, purchased factory in Hammondville

1896–1965	Bryce Brothers, factory in Mt. Pleasant
1965–	Lenox Co.

James Bryce, born in Scotland in 1812, came with his family to the United States when he was 5 years old. They lived in Philadelphia for about two years then moved west and settled in Pittsburgh. James was indentured to Bakewell, Page & Bakewell in 1827 at age 15. As a result of an economic panic in the late 1830s, the Bakewell factory closed temporarily in 1840 and James turned to work in the grocery business. He returned to glass blowing in 1845 when he secured a position with Mulvany and Ledlie.

Dun records indicate that James established the firm, Bryce, McKee and Co., in 1850 with his brothers Robert and John Bryce, and the McKee brothers Frederick and James. The deed of sale for the lot at Wharton and 21st streets on the South Side includes names of the other shareholders: William F. Hartley, Peter M. Reid, Thomas Adams, John A. H. Carson, Samuel Charters, James Reddick, Matthew Lieler (or Seibler) Joseph Doyle, John Floyd, Richard Floyd, and Edward Hazelton.

In 1854, the McKee brothers withdrew when their father set them up in their own business. Two new partners bought into the company — Joseph Richards and William T. Hartley, and the firm became Bryce, Richards and Co. In 1865, Richards and Hartley left to form their own business and were replaced by W. and H. Walker, and firm changed its name to Bryce, Walker and Co. It finally became Bryce Brothers in 1882 when the Walkers sold out their interest. The deed notes that interest in the parcel was sold by Margaret Walker because William Walker had been "declared a lunatic." Further information on Mr. Walker's condition could not be found.

In 1879, John Bryce withdrew from the firm and joined his son Charles, John Higbee, and Joseph Doyle to form Bryce Higbee in Homestead, 5 miles southeast of Pittsburgh. Around the turn of the century their firm's name was changed to J. B. Higbee Glass Co. and was moved to Bridgeville, Pa.

Bryce Brothers joined the U.S. Glass trust in 1891 as Factory B, and Andrew Bryce became its secretary. In 1893, Bryce Brothers was reorganized when Andrew and J. McDonald Bryce withdrew from U. S. Glass and purchased a bankrupt factory in Hammondville, Pa. Three years later, in 1896, the firm built a new factory in Mt. Pleasant.

Bryce Brothers manufactured tableware, lamps, apothecary wares, and bottles, and was known for dozens of pressed glass patterns including Roman Rosette, Ribbon Candy, and Ribbed Palm or Sprig. It also held a number of design patents, such as Diamond Sunburst, Thistle, and Strawberry. The Bryce Brothers catalog for 1964 features dozens of pieces of stemware as well as goblets, vases, candy jars, and ashtrays.

Lenox's purchase of the company led to a new glass factory complex in Mt. Pleasant which allows Lenox to produce fine crystal tableware and giftware that coordinates with its china.

CHALLINOR TAYLOR

1864–70	Pittsburgh Glass Manufacturing Co.
1870	Challinor, McCombs
1871–1883	Challinor, Hogan and Co.
1884–1891	Challinor Taylor, Tarentum, Pa.
1891	Joined U.S. Glass Co. as Factory C

Pittsburgh Glass Manufacturing Co. began operations by purchasing 10 lots in Birmingham (now Pittsburgh's South Side) at Washington (now Sarah) Street at S. Eighth Street. The book *Manufacturers and Manufacturies* notes that the company was founded as a joint stock company with 40 employees making tableware and lamp chimneys. The lots were sold in August 1869 to McCombs Townsend and Co. and the city directory for 1870 lists the firm's name as Challinor, McCombs. Norris McCombs is variously listed as the treasurer of the Pittsburgh Glass Manufacturing Co. and as a gentleman living in Pittsburgh's East End. In January of 1870, the property was sold to David Challinor, Edward Hogan, James Fawcett, Lucas Minehart, and David Taylor. The firm name then became Challinor, Hogan and Co. In 1871, the factory's capacity was doubled; specialties then were lamp chimneys, silvered glassware, and candy jars.

David Challinor was among the many glassmen who worked for Bakewells. He also worked many years for Mulvany and Ledlie. His partner, Edward Hogan, also apprenticed with Mulvany. On June 1, 1886, Challinor received a patent for variegated glassware, a blend of white and colored glass which, when pressed, formed a marbled or swirled pattern. Challinor Hogan manufactured tableware, novelties such as match safes, and latticework plates and compotes. Like Atterbury, the company also produced a line of animal covered dishes in the shape of a hen, rooster, eagle, swan, duck, and fish.

In 1883, Challinor dissolved the partnership with Hogan and joined with David Taylor to form Challinor Taylor. Lured by inexpensive, open land and natural gas for furnaces, they joined the late 19th century exodus from Pittsburgh and built a new factory in Tarentum, about 10 miles up the Allegheny, northeast of the city. The firm remained there until joining the U.S. Glass Co. as Factory C.

CHAMBERS & MCKEE

1880–1897	Chambers & McKee
1899–1958	American Window Glass Co.
1958–1970	American St. Gobain Corp.
1970–1988	ASG Industries, Inc.
1988–1993	General Glass Industries, Inc.

In 1887, H. Sellers McKee and James A. Chambers purchased a tract of land in the Grapeville area of Westmoreland County, about 25 miles east of Pittsburgh, where they erected a large window glass factory. The new factory was fully integrated and included the first continuous tank installed in the United States. Instead of melting and working a new batch each day, the new tank continuously melted the raw ingredients, allowing the company to work three consecutive 8-hour shifts.

In 1899, Chambers organized the American Window Glass Co. and bought out 41 window glass companies, including the works of Chambers & McKee. Chambers also financed the research and development of the Lubbers cylinder machine, which was developed by one of Chambers' window glass flatteners. The technology was again replaced 20 years later by sheet-drawn processes.

The company was purchased by the American St. Gobain Corp. in 1958 and by ASG Industries in 1970. The firm traded hands again in 1988, when the factory was purchased by General Glass Industries, which produced flat glass. GGI declared bankruptcy in 1993. In 1997, demolition of the plant began, the first step toward the site's redevelopment as an industrial park. Archival materials from the factory are in the collections of the Historical Society of Western Pennsylvania.

CONSOLIDATED LAMP & GLASS CO.

1894–1895	Factory in Fostoria, Ohio
1896–1964	Factory in Coraopolis, Pa.

When Wallace and McAfee Co. merged with Fostoria Shade and Lamp Co. in 1893, it became Consolidated Lamp and Glass Co., the largest lamp, globe, and shade works in the United States. The new company commenced business on January 1, 1894, with a factory in Fostoria, Ohio, and headquarters at 918-920 Penn Avenue in Pittsburgh. The November 22, 1893, issue of *China, Glass & Lamps* reported that F.G. Wallace became president of Consolidated and the other officers were J.B. Graham as secretary, Joseph G. Walter as treasurer, and Nicholas Kopp as manager. In 1896, after the Fostoria plant burned down, Consolidated moved its factory to a 7-acre tract in Coraopolis.

A c. 1905 poster indicates that Consolidated produced 400 dozen decorated lamps per day. It also produced tableware and art lines and in the 1920s and 1930s introduced Martele (1926), Santa Maria (1926), Catalonian (1927), Florentine (1927), Ruba Rombic (1928), and Line 700 (1929). The *Coraopolis Record* stated that the company was a pioneer in the manufacture of cerise (red) and other colored glass. According to Jack D. Wilson, in *Phoenix and Consolidated Art Glass, 1926-1980*, Nicholas Kopp deserves much of the credit for Cosolidated's late 19th century satin glass, ruby glass, cased glass, and straw opalescent glass. A master of cased glasswork, he originally worked in the Fostoria plant and moved to Coraopolis to remain with Consolidated, before he started his own company in 1899.

The Depression shut down Consolidated from April 2, 1932, until March 1936. During that time, some of their molds were used by the Phoenix Glass Co. in nearby Monaca, Pa. New management reopened Consolidated, and in 1956 the McCune family sold the company to brothers named Dietz. The company produced decorated milk glass called Concora as well as the Regent line. Fire severely damaged the factory in 1963, and it closed the next year.

CUNNINGHAM & CO.

1845	Wilson Cunningham and George Whitten Jackson
1849–1857	W. Cunningham & Co., Pittsburgh City Glass Works
1857–1864	Cunninghams & Co.
1865–1878	Cunninghams & Ihmsen
1878	Cunninghams & Co., 26th and Jane streets
1880–1931	D.O. Cunningham, 22nd and Jane streets

Wilson Cunningham was born in Allegheny County in 1812. At age 12, he went to work for the glass company Wendt, Ensell & Ihmsen. Cunningham began blowing glass at 16 and continued with the firm until he was 27. For the next decade he tried his hand at selling Pittsburgh goods on the Ohio and Mississippi rivers, but he returned to the glass trade in the 1840s. According to an early writer on Pittsburgh glass, Wilson Cunningham first ventured into glass manufacturing when he and partner George Whitten Jackson built a bottle and window glass factory on Water Street in 1845. However, the city directory for 1847 lists Wilson Cunningham as a trader in Birmingham, and Jackson as a soap and candle maker on Fourth Avenue.

Within a few years, Wilson was joined by brothers Robert and Dominic Wilson and George Duncan, and the firm name became W. Cunningham & Co. Robert Cunningham first entered the glass trade at 16 when he learned the art of blowing window glass from John McKee. After four years with the firm, he left to accompany his brother to travel and sell between Pittsburgh and New Orleans. Dominic Ihmsen, scion of another prominent glassmaking family, joined the Cunninghams in 1857.

Dominic O. Cunningham, son of Wilson, was born in 1834. He began working for the family business at 16 as a bookkeeper. In 1864, he became a principal in the firm when he bought out George Duncan's interest.

Cunningham made a wide variety of items in its nearly 100-year history. During the Gold Rush in 1859, it was among the many firms to manufacture the popular Pikes Peak flasks. In an 1872 city directory ad, the company touted its products as glassware, flasks, and demijohns, wine, brandy and soda water bottles, and the "celebrated Queen and Hero" fruit jars. Two years later, Cunninghams was advertising druggist's glass, American plate glass, railroad car glass, and headlights.

The 1879 book *Industries of Pittsburgh* states that Cunnigham's three extensive factories made it the largest glassworks in the United States. Dominic Cunningham became the sole owner the following year. Bottles made at the factory are often marked "DOC" along the body near the base. All-Pak, a distributor, purchased the company in 1931.

DOYLE & CO.

1866–1882	Doyle & Co.
1868	Second plant at 10th and Washington (now Sarah) streets, Birmingham
1891	U.S. Glass Co., Factory P

Partners Joseph Doyle, William Doyle, William Beck, and John McCutcheon founded the company at 10th and Bingham streets in Birmingham. To expand operations two years later, they purchased a parcel from Alexander King two blocks away. In the 1869 city directory, the firm advertised being manufacturers of French Flint Glass, making table sets, tumblers, goblets, chimneys, and jars with "special attention given to annealed sun chimneys." An undated (c. 1875) ad also touted a specialty in "Patent Tin Top Jellies." The *Crockery Journal* noted in 1875 that Doyle's principal markets were in the West, South, and Canada.

In 1881, a subsidiary, Doyle Sons & Co., opened in Monaca, Pa., to manufacture lamp chimneys. After operating for a few years, the plant was offered for sale. According to John and Elizabeth Welker in *Pressed Glass in America*, the plant was purchased by Phoenix Glass Co. in 1890.

Deeds indicate that in 1882, nine years before it became Factory P of U.S. Glass Co., the original plant at 10th and Bingham was sold to H. W. Oliver, Jr., of Oliver Iron and Steel.

Like many companies, Doyle often used only numbers to identify its pressed pattern glassware. Collectors know some of its patterns as Grape and Festoon with Shield, Snail, and Excelsior. Doyle also made a Centennial salt in the form of a cracked Liberty Bell.

DUNCAN & MILLER GLASS CO.

1874–1893	George Duncan & Sons
1891–92	Joined U.S. Glass Co.
1893–1900	George Duncan's Sons & Co.
1900–1955	Duncan & Miller Glass Co.
1955	Bought by U.S. Glass Co.

In the 1860s, George Duncan was associated with a number of Pittsburgh area businesses, including the glass firm Ripley & Co. Duncan is listed in the Pittsburgh city directory for 1867/68 as being "of Ripley & Co. and McKnight & Co." Duncan bought out Ripley & Co. in 1874 and joined with sons James E. and Harry B., and son-in-law A. H. Heisey to form George Duncan & Sons. That same year, Duncan offered J. Ernest Miller a position as a designer. An experienced mold-maker, Miller designed the famous Three Face, a stem or knob comprised of three women's faces, using his wife as a model. Duncan's illustrated catalog for 1874 pictures its wide variety of wares including goblets, tumblers, pitchers, compotes, decanters, lamps, and novelties. George Duncan died in 1877 and was succeeded by his son, James Duncan.

The firm reluctantly joined the United States Glass Co. in 1891; however, the plant burned the following year. Duncan took advantage of the situation and moved the company to Washington, Pa., where, in January 1893, work began at the new factory. In November 1900, the firm was incorporated as the Duncan & Miller Glass Co., when designer J. Edward Miller joined Mrs. James E. Duncan, Sr., James E. Duncan Jr., Andrew P. Duncan, and Harry B. Duncan. The firm continued to manufacture all varieties of tableware.

Duncan & Miller stopped making glass in 1955, when U.S. Glass acquired it. The factory's molds and machinery were moved to plants in Tiffin, Ohio, and Glassport, Pa.; a "Duncan Division" was carried on at those two factories. The factory building in Washington was sold to Andy Brothers, a firm that recapped tires. Before the new company could begin operations, the building burned in a fire on June 29, 1956.

H.C. FRY GLASS CO.

1901–1902	Rochester Glass Co.
1902–1933	H.C. Fry Glass Co.
1934	Plant leased by Libbey Glass Co.

Before beginning the glass company that bore his name, Henry Clay Fry had a long association with the industry. He learned the business while serving as a principal in several Pittsburgh firms, and then as an agent and manager for the O'Hara Glassworks. In 1872, he was one of the founders and president of Rochester Tumbler. The company became one of the largest pressed glass producers in the world, employing 1,100 people at its height and producing over a half-million pieces of glass a week. In 1899, the company became part of the National Glass Co. trust and Fry became the president. In 1901, he and his sons began the independent concern known best as the Fry Glass Co.

Though revered for rich cut glass and blanks for glass cutting, as well as fine blown glass, the company also produced a line of ovenware, made tableware and kitchenware, did some industrial products such as insulators and lenses, made chemical glassware, heat-resistant stove doors, and, through a separate concern, glass containers for gasoline pumps. Blown glass with decorative threading done by Fry has been confused with Steuben, and its art line of Foval glass and acid-etched decorations are widely sought. The company struggled financially during the Depression of the 1930s and closed in 1933. Libbey briefly leased the factory in the 1930s.

GLENSHAW GLASS CO.

1895–	Glenshaw Glass Co.

An investment of $600 each by John M. Farrell, John Stehle, John Jacob Altmeyer, and John Jacob Beck provided the capital for this bottle manufacturer. The original factory was across the street from where the current plant now stands along Route 8 (once called Butler Plank Road) in Glenshaw, a few miles north of Pittsburgh. The original production line was flasks, but the company gradually expanded into a wide range of bottles, including soda, beer, and water bottles, packer's and fruit jars, and food and condiment containers. Shortly after the founding, John Jacob Meyer became a partner, and eventually the Berner family would also invest in the plant.

The company suffered a number of fires during its first 30 years but always rebuilt and continued production. By 1948, the plant had the capacity to turn out 175 tons of glass a day; in the 1950s, that figure increased by 25 percent. In 1960, Glenshaw built a plant in Orangeburg, N.Y., and added a mould shop to the Pittsburgh works. A downturn in business in the 1980s led to the closing and sale of the Orangeburg plant.

In the late 1980s, Glenshaw, which had remained under the management of the descendants of the early partners, was sold to G&G Investments, Inc., led by John Ghaznavi, a recent Iranian immigrant who is said to have come to America with only a few hundred dollars. Changes in management and improvements in furnaces and equipment led to a turnaround. The company also acquired controlling interest in Consumers Packaging of Canada and in 1997, purchased 11 plants of the former Anchor Glass Container Corp. Current product lines include Mrs. Butterworth syrup bottles, Arizona Ice Tea bottles, Real Lemon bottles and a variety of beverage containers. The 1 million bottles a day turned out at the original factory in Glenshaw can be identified by the trademark "G" in a square.

J.T. & A. Hamilton

c.1880–1943   J.T. & A. Hamilton
by 1888   Second plant in Butler, Pa.
1943–1947   Seaboard Glass Bottle Co.

J.T. & A. Hamilton first appeared in the Pittsburgh city directories in 1881 with a factory at 26th and Railroad streets. J.T. Hamilton was a native Pittsburgher and is described as having been "brought up in the industry" and as "one of the foremost authorities therein to be found in the United States." The company manufactured flasks, prescription vials, and bottles, including those for Pittsburgh Brewing Co. The Pittsburgh plant was handily situated on the Allegheny Valley Railroad line, with direct switch connection to facilitate shipping of raw materials and product. As a director of the New York and Cleveland Gas Coal Co., Hamilton may have been one of his own best customers. J.T. Hamilton was also president of the Standard Plate Co. and a director of the Third National Bank in Pittsburgh.

An 1896 report, *Pittsburgh of Today*, describes two 12-pot furnaces on premises covering 120 by 288 feet, and it depicts the 4-acre Butler plant as "one of the most extensive and best equipped bottle works in America." Together, the plants employed about 300 workers. In 1898, Simonds & Wainwright Audit Co. of New York's report on flint glass bottling plants assigns a value of

$76,429 to the firm, the fourth largest in the survey.

The factory became the Seaboard Glass Bottle Co. in 1943 with J. T. Hamilton, Jr., as the vice president and plant manager. The *National Glass Budget's* annual directory of glass factories lists Seaboard for the last time in 1947.

C. IHMSEN & CO.

c.1812–c.1822   Beltzhoover, Wendt & Co.
c.1822–1836   Sutton, Wendt & Co.
1836–c.1839   Whitehead, Ihmsen & Phillips
1836–1850   C. Ihmsen & Co. (absorbed into C. Ihmsen)
1846–1850   Young, Ihmsen & Plunkett
1850–1855   C. Ihmsen
1850–1855   C. Ihmsen & Co.
1855–1885   C. Ihmsen & Sons
1885–1895   Ihmsen & Co.

Like many other Pittsburgh glass businesses, the roots of the Ihmsen family concerns can be traced to James O'Hara's Pittsburgh Glass Works. An 1812 contract documents the formation of a partnership between three investors and five glassworkers including Charles Ihmsen, a German immigrant. The firm, reportedly named for the investors, Beltzhoover, Wendt & Co., made window glass and hollowware.

Charles Ihmsen's eldest son, William, began his own glassworks at Williamsport on the Monongahela River in the 1820s. The Historical Society of Western Pennsylvania has a flask from that factory marked "W. Ihmsen, Williamsport." However, it is the younger Ihmsen boy, Christian, who had the most significant impact on glassmaking. After his father died in 1828, Christian took his place in the firm then called Sutton, Wendt & Co. By 1836, he was a partner in four glass factories. C. Ihmsen & Co. owned the two Birmingham Vial and Window Glass Factories. (It seems possible that this was the successor to Sutton, Wendt & Co., which is said to have made window glass and hollowware.) Another partnership, Whitehead, Ihmsen & Phillips, owned the two Pennsylvania Flint and Black Glass factories.

According to the 1837 Pittsburgh city directory, the Ihmsen black glass factory employed 15 blowers from Bristol, England. The vial factory made "112,600 gross of vials from one half drahn (sic) to 16 ounces, and 60 gross of flasks, oil bottles & hollowware." The window glass factory made windows as large as 24" x 30", which they described as "very little inferior to the best crown glass." Flint glassware included cut, plain, and pressed products.

The 1849 Dun records noted that Christian Ihmsen was one of Pittsburgh's most substantial citizens and that he had given security for a new firm — Young, Ihmsen & Plunkett, formed in 1846. (Typical of the constant activity in Pittsburgh glass partnerships, Whitehead seems to have formed another firm, Whitehead, Sproul & Co., in Birmingham around 1839, and Phillips is also believed to have founded his own glasshouse in 1840.) By 1850, Young, Ihmsen and Plunkett had become C. Ihmsen. Interestingly, as early as 1844, only "C. Ihmsen" is listed in the Pittsburgh city directory. In the 1847 directory, C. Ihmsen advertised window glass "common and Patent, being an imitation of crown or Plate Glass," vials, bottles, jars, black porter and wine bottles, demijohns, and flint (lead) glass. These listings suggest that while behind-the-scenes ownership changes occurred, Ihmsen marketed the products of different factories under one name.

Around 1851, Christian Ihmsen's son Charles T. Ihmsen became involved in the glass business when he partnered with A.I. Ulam in a venture that succeeded Ledlie & Ulam. Ihmsen & Ulam advertised in the 1859 city directory that their Mulvany Glass Works made "Flint Glass of Every Description." By 1862, the firm had disappeared from Pittsburgh directories.

In 1855, Christian Ihmsen partnered with his two sons, Charles T. and William Ihmsen, as well as F. M'Gowin, in the firm of C. Ihmsen & Co. They owned five factories that were "prepared to furnish all articles made of glass." The name changed to C. Ihmsen & Sons soon after when a third son joined the business. (Another Ihmsen relative, Dominick, was involved in the glass firm Cunninghams & Co.) Christian Ihmsen died in 1862, and it appears that the company ceased manufacturing window glass at this time. His sons operated the firm under his name until 1885, when it was absorbed into Ihmsen Glass & Co. The firm went out of business in 1895.

JEANNETTE SPECIALTY GLASS

c. 1900–1910	Empire Glass Co.
1910–1991	Jeannette Shade & Novelty Co.
1991–	Jeannette Specialty Glass

This was another of the companies that took advantage of abundant stores of natural gas and available land in Westmoreland County at its founding. Early on, the company produced lamp globes, shades, and chimneys. After 1910, the company still produced glass but also began providing molds to other glass companies. Its glass output was widely varied — opal glass lighting for schools and businesses, glass globes for gasoline pumps, and advertising pieces for dairies and cigar and drug stores. Today, the company concentrates on lighting for residential and commercial uses, and also manufactures lens refractors, traffic signals, and specialty mold items.

KING, SON & CO.

1859	Cascade Glass Works established by Johnson, King & Co.
1865–1869	Johnson, King & Co.
1869–1880	King, Son & Co.
1880–1884	King Glass Co.
1884–1888	King, Son & Co.
1888–1891	King Glass Co.
1891	Joined U.S. Glass Co. as Factory K

The original location of Cascade Glass Works in Birmingham (now Pittsburgh's South Side) was at 18th and Meadow streets. When it purchased three additional lots in October 1869, 16 names were listed on the deed record as buyers: Ralph Johnson, James Johnson, David C. King, W. King, Gregory Fox, Philip Goodbub, Francis A. Fisher, Jacob Zimmer, Charles Zimmers, J. M. Wilker, Fredolin Myer, George Steinmeyer, Henry Louzettle, Frederick Smunk, Henry Freise, and George Irwin. By 1869, the plant had two 10-pot furnaces and 100 workers. The name change in 1869 occurred when the son of David C. King, William C. King, joined the firm. The elder King died in 1874. In 1879, the firm endured a labor strike. A 1942 retrospective on the South Side's glass industry noted that the factory's nickname was "Fox's Place."

By 1880, 110 workers were employed at King Glass. In the same year that colored glass was introduced to the product line (1884), fire destroyed the plant and the company was again reorganized as King, Son & Co. The managers at this time were Wm. C. King, George B. Swift, Addison H. Litch, and John L. Lyon. That same year, the firm also bought the burned factory of

Crystal Glass Co. in Bridgeport, Ohio. By 1886, the South Side operation employed 325 workers, with two furnaces — one 14-pot and an 11-pot.

The partnership was again dissolved in 1888 and went back to the name King Glass Co., with major shareholders Charles Zimmers and Henry Freese. George Swift resigned in 1889 and went with Greensburg Glass Co., dying the year before the company joined U.S. Glass as Factory K.

An article in the Fall 1986 issue of *The Glass Club Bulletin* describes lamps made by King to be of "very good quality colorless glass as well as optic molded and opalescent colored glass." Over the firm's long history, King, Son & Co. manufactured crystal glassware, tableware, bar ware, patent glass covers, candy jars, jelly jars, ring jars, and colored flint glass. Its products were sold across the nation, in Canada, and in South America.

KOPP GLASS INC.

1899–1901	Kopp Glass Co.
1901–1926	Pittsburgh Lamp, Brass and Glass Co.
1926–	Kopp Glass Inc.

Nicholas Kopp was the founding partner and guiding light of Kopp Glass. A renowned chemist or "color man," he had already made his mark in the glass world at Fostoria and Consolidated when he started a new company that bore his name in Swissvale, Pa. In a former automobile plant nestled next to the railroad tracks, the company turned out beautiful lamps and some tableware. In 1901, the company took on new partners and reorganized as Pittsburgh Lamp, Brass and Glass Co., specializing in lamps and lighting in an array of colors and decorations.

The company also began producing railroad signal lights in the selenium red developed by Kopp in the 1890s. In 1926, PLB&G went bankrupt and the company again took the Kopp name. Signals and lenses became an increasingly important part of the business, though the company continued to produce domestic lighting fixtures, lamps and vases, including the Modernistic line, through the 1930s. Today the company is a world leader in the production of lenses, traffic signals, and airport and aircraft lighting.

MACBETH-EVANS GLASS CO.

1899–1936	Macbeth-Evans Glass Co.
1936–1998	Corning Glass Works
1998–	Purchased by New York investment firm Kohlberg Kravis Roberts & Co.

Economic necessity spawned this company's creation in 1899 when two Pittsburgh firms, the Thos. Evans Co. and the George A. Macbeth Co., merged. Both men realized that the invention of an automatic blowing machine for lamp chimneys would drive them out of the glassblowing business unless they pooled resources to purchase the patented technology; the price tag was $300,000 each. Macbeth-Evans had plants in Pittsburgh (at both 18th and Josephine streets and 27th and Josephine on the South Side), Charleroi, and in Elwood and Marion, Indiana. The company was the largest producer of lamp chimneys in the world. As late as 1936, it still turned out 6 million a year. Another specialty was illuminating and optical glass; the firm made the searchlights for the Panama Canal, lighthouse lenses, streetlights, railway signals, lanterns, headlight lenses for Ford automobiles, laboratory glass, and a variety of other industrial products. In the 1920s, the company began producing machine-made tableware in a variety of colors with two of the better-known patterns being American Sweetheart and Dogwood. The company also produced an opalescent line known as Monax. After merging with Corning Glass in 1936, primary production at the Charleroi plant was Pyrex ovenware.

MCCULLY & CO.

1829–1832	Hay & McCully
early 1830s	McCully & Co.
1840–1899	Wm. McCully & Co.

Like many men in the trade, William McCully learned the art of glassblowing as an apprentice at the Bakewell factory. He continued as a journeyman at O'Hara's Pittsburgh Glass Works. In about 1830, McCully joined with John Hay to erect a factory on Railroad and 19th streets. The partnership dissolved in 1832, and the following year McCully built a factory at 16th Street and Liberty Avenue to manufacture bottles. McCully teamed with Frederick Lorenz in the early 1830s to found McCully & Co. (McKearin states 1836, Welker states 1830-32.) Next, according to Welker, Wm. McCully & Co. was organized in 1840-41 with partners William McCully, Frederick Lorenz, Thomas Wightman, and A.W. Buchanan. This partnership dissolved 10 years later when McCully was joined by his son, John. Other family members were taken in when sons-in-law Mark Watson and John King came on board, in 1852 and 1855 respectively. They were later joined by John McKelvey and Robert McClardy. After McCully's death in 1869, the remaining four partners carried on under the same name.

McCully operated a number of factories including the Pittsburgh, Phoenix, Empire, Sligo, and Mastodon Glass Works. An ad in the Pittsburgh city directory for 1867/68 announced that the firm made bottles, vials, demijohns, green glassware, and window glass. Wilson and McKearin note that there are several marked "Wm. & McCully" flasks. The firm was last listed in Pittsburgh city directories in 1909.

MCKEE GLASS CO.

1850–1853	F.&J. McKee
1853–1860	McKee Brothers (or McKee & Brother)
1860–1888	McKee & Brothers
1888–1899	McKee & Brothers (Jeannette)
1899–1904	National Glass Co. as McKee & Bros. Glass Works
1904–1908	McKee Jeannette Glass Co.
1908–1951	McKee Glass Co.
1951–1961	Division of Thatcher Mfg. Co.
1961–1971	Purchased by Jeannette Glass Co.
1971–1983?	Jeannette Corp.

The name McKee has meant glass in Western Pennsylvania since the 1850s. Two brothers, Frederick and James McKee, founded the factory on Pittsburgh's South Side on what was then Clifton Street between 18th and 19th streets. The company, known first as F.&J. McKee, was one of the largest producers of flint glass in the United States, as well as a producer of vials, bottles, and window glass.

In 1888, the Pittsburgh works was sold to King Glass Co. and H. Sellers McKee relocated the factory to a tract of farmland he had purchased with fellow South Side glassman James Chambers in Westmoreland County. There they built more than just a glass factory, they built a town. Named Jeannette, for McKee's wife, the town became known as "America's glass city." McKee and Chambers built a window glass and a tableware factory, as well as homes for glassworkers on Fifth and Sixth avenues, businesses, and even a bank.

The McKee factory sprawled across nearly 5 acres. The company produced patterned tableware and introduced a line of milk glass. Some McKee pieces from this period are marked with a script logo that reads "McKee."

At the turn of the century, the factory introduced it's PRESCUT line (some pieces being marked with that name), which was pressed glassed made to mimic the rich cut glass of the period. The line is sometimes known as "TEC ware," as patterns had names such as Aztec and Yutec. During that time, the company also made headlights for Ford automobiles.

In the 1920s and '30s, the company made a wide range of Depression Era tableware, introducing lines such as the Laurel and Lenox dinnerware. It also produced kitchenware in a range of opaque colors — Jade Green, Skokie green, Chalaine blue, and Seville yellow. Glasbake ovenware was a staple of the line for much of the 20th century. The company marked some of these wares "McK" in a circle.

Innovative designers often brought ideas to McKee. In the late 1920s, illustrator Tony Sarg (known for his work at the *Saturday Evening Post*) designed a decanter set produced by McKee known as the Jolly Golfer. The decanter is shaped like a golfer, with each cup like the golfer's head; the figures' removable hats serve as coasters. Other innovative designs from the 1930s include the Art Nude Vase, the Bottoms Up and Bottoms Down tumblers and mugs, and the Danse De Lumiere lamp that borrowed directly from a Lalique design.

McKee remained in business in a partnership first with Thatcher Glass in the 1950s and then with the Jeannette Glass Co. The factory closed in the 1980s. The abandoned factory still stands in Jeannette.

MULVANY AND LEDLIE

c.1832–1845	O'Leary, Mulvany & Co., Birmingham Flint Glass Co.
1845–1850	Mulvany & Ledlie
1850–1858	Ledlie & Ulam
1858–1860	Ihmsen & Ulam, Mulvany Glass Works

Birmingham Flint Glass Co. was founded by William O'Leary, a glass cutter, and Patrick Mulvany, a cabinet maker. According to *Pressed Glass in America* (Welker), the factory was located in Birmingham (now Pittsburgh's South Side) beside the Monongahela River at 16th Street. In 1845, O'Leary left the firm and James Ekin Ledlie joined the company. Ledlie apparently brought capital rather than glassmaking expertise to the enterprise. He is listed in the 1837 city directory as a commission merchant as well as a member of the board of directors of the Pittsburgh Exchange Bank. An ad for Mulvany & Ledlie in the 1850 city directory describes them as manufacturers of "cut, moulded & plain flint and fancy colored glassware, and dealers in all kinds of window glass, flasks, vials & bottles." The Historical Society of Western Pennsylvania has in its collection a Mulvany & Ledlie compote cut in panels with amethyst overlay.

Patrick Mulvany died in 1854, a few years after withdrawing from the firm. A. T. Ulam, who joined in 1850, was Mulvany's son-in-law. According to *Pressed Glass in America*, Ledlie died in 1858 and Charles Ihmsen purchased his interest, but Ledlie may have simply retired: a genealogy of the Ledlie and William Moody families records that James Ledlie retired "about the time of the Civil War" and died at age 85 in 1891. Financial troubles forced the factory's closing in 1860.

PHOENIX GLASS CO.

1880–1970	Phoenix Glass Co.
1970	Purchased by Anchor Hocking Corp.

The Phoenix Glass Co. founder was Andrew Howard, in Phillipsburg (now Monaca), Pa. An article in the *Beaver Argus* on June 16, 1880, noted that the company intended to manufacture lamp chimneys. E.D. Dithridge, whose family was long associated with the manufacture of lamp chimneys, became the production manager. Soon Phoenix expanded its line to include lamp shades and globes.

In 1883, Phoenix contracted with English glassmaker Joseph Webb to make "various colored glasses and... special novelties and shapes from same." Webb's talents enabled Phoenix to break into the art glass field. During his 11 years with the company, Webb received three patents for mother-of-pearl satin glass. Letterhead from 1887 describes the company as "manufacturers of Flint, Colored and Venetian Glass Ware, in Table, Gas and Kerosene Goods." Phoenix continued to focus on lighting until the 1930s, when it turned to decorative art glass.

In the early 1930s, Kenneth Haley, son of designer Reuben Haley, was employed at Phoenix. He introduced its "Sculptured Artware" line. These bore a paper label with a bird in a circle with the words "Phoenix" and "Sculptured Artware." This line of vases and other home decorating items was very three-dimensional and included floral motifs, flying geese, and cameos. When neighboring Consolidated Lamp & Glass temporarily shut down during the Depression, Phoenix borrowed some of the molds from the latter's Martele line.

Like many factories, Phoenix became a defense plant during WW II, supplying glass for the armed services. It returned to decorative glassware after the war. The company was purchased by Anchor Hocking in 1970, for whom it manufactured a wide range of lighting components. Phoenix is still owned by Anchor's parent, Newell Co.

PPG INDUSTRIES, INC.

1880–1883	New York City Plate Glass Co.
1883–1968	Pittsburgh Plate Glass Co.
1968–	PPG Industries, Inc.

In 1880, entrepreneur Capt. John B. Ford and railroad magnate John Pitcairn began building a plant for the manufacture of plate glass at Creighton, northeast of Pittsburgh along the Allegheny River. The company was reincorporated and renamed three years later. During the 1880s, the company also added plants in Ford City (named for Capt. Ford). In 1895, the corporate headquarters were situated in Pittsburgh, where they remain to this day. At that time, the company was capable of producing 20 million square-feet of plate glass a year, and became a major supplier to the American market. Ford and Pitcairn parted ways in 1896, and Ford went on to found the Edward Ford Plate Glass Co. of Toledo (now Libbey-Owens-Ford Glass Co.)

In 1900, Pitcairn diversified the company and it began to produce and distribute paints and brushes. The company also built a factory in Belgium and two flat glass plants in the United States. With an international presence, a diversified product line, and its own distribution system, company fortunes increased. The addition of a research and development facility at Creighton in

1910 added further potential for new products and new markets.

Between 1900 and 1920, two changes in American life — the widespread production of the automobile and the building of skyscrapers — increased the demand for flat glass. Pittsburgh Plate Glass developed a method for drawing flat glass in sheets that allowed it to greatly increase volume for serving the new markets. Its 1923 *Yearbook* details the amazing array of products manufactured or sold by Pittsburgh Plate Glass during this period. In 1934, the company introduced its first "environmental" glass for architecture — heat-absorbing Solex glass. During World War II, the company also developed new glass for use in aircraft, and after the war, profited from its R&D work with the relatively new substance of fiberglass.

In 1963, PPG became the first American company licensed to use British float glass technology. Its facility in Meadville, Pa., has the capacity to produce 1 million square-feet of float glass a day, enough for 20,000 automobiles. The company operates glass plants around the country and the world, is among the top four world producers of float glass, and is the world's second largest producer of continuous-strand fiberglass.

RIPLEY & CO.

1865–1891	Ripley & Co.
1891	Joined United States Glass Co. as Factory F

In October 1865, Daniel Campbell Ripley, Sr., joined with Thomas Coffin, Ira Coffin, Jacob Strickler, John Strickler, and Nicholas Kunzler to establish Ripley & Co. They purchased property on Pittsburgh's South Side along Carson between 10th and 11th streets from another glass family, the Ihmsens. The factory was called the Tremont Glass Works. An ad in the 1867/68 Pittsburgh city directory states that the firm manufactured "Flint glass, tumblers, goblets, bowls, dishes, etc." By 1870, several of the original partners had withdrawn from the business and Daniel C. Ripley, Sr., died. The remaining partners, D.C. Ripley, Jr., George Duncan, and Jacob Strickler, stayed together until 1874 when Duncan bought out the company and created George Duncan & Sons.

D.C. Ripley, Jr., joined with a new partner John Stevenson and purchased a lot across from the Bakewell, Pears factory on Bingham between Eighth and Ninth streets. They built a new factory and began operations again as Ripley & Co. The Fall 1988 issue of *The Illuminator* notes that 11 patents were issued to the Ripleys, most of them for lamps. Ripley was apparently fond of double handles and double fonts, which made tableware and lamps easier to pass, as a number of their items had this feature. Among Ripley's well known lamps are the Wedding lamp and the Baptismal font.

In 1891, Ripley & Co. joined the United States Glass Co. as Factory F with D.C. Ripley, Jr. as the first president. Initially, the main offices were housed in the Ripley factory. In August 1909, Ripley resigned from U.S. Glass and formed another Ripley & Co. in Connellsville. An Aug. 23, 1931 *Pittsburgh Press* article noted that the old Ripley factory on the South Side was being dismantled.

ROCHESTER TUMBLER CO.

1872–1900	Rochester Tumbler Co.
1900–1904	Joined National Glass Co. as Rochester Glass works
1904–1918	Plant leased to new corporation again known as Rochester Tumbler Co.
1918	Purchased by General Electric, for Rochester Bulb Co.

The Rochester Tumbler Co. was established with Henry Clay Fry as president and Jesse H. Lippencott as treasurer. The *Pennsylvania Historical Review* of 1886 states that the company had the capacity to turn out over 45,000 dozen tumblers per week — pressed and cut, colored and plain — and was the largest pressed glass works in the world. This figure was increased to 75,000 dozen in the 1890s. Their market was worldwide. The company had agencies in major cities throughout the U.S. and exported its wares to South America, Europe, Australia, and South Africa.

At the turn of the century, the firm joined the National Glass Co. as the Rochester Glass Works and H. C. Fry served as the first president. In February 1901, the factory was destroyed by fire, but it was rebuilt the following year.

In 1904, National Glass leased the plant to a new corporation also known as Rochester Tumbler. The plant was purchased in 1918 by

General Electric, which operated it as the Rochester Bulb Co.

L.E. SMITH GLASS CO.

1907–   L. E. Smith Glass Co.

L.E. Smith was founded by Louis E. Smith and Thomas E. Wible as a glass decorating firm. In 1909, they purchased the Anchor Glass plant in Mt. Pleasant and began to manufacture mustard containers and other tableware. Fire destroyed the factory in April 1913, but the equipment survived the blaze, so employees returned to work within days and continued to work in the open air while the factory was rebuilt.

For a time after the new factory was erected, L.E. Smith produced vault lights — glass blocks used in buildings and sidewalks that let light into underground areas. During the 1920s, L.E. Smith made headlight lenses for Ford Motor Co. and also manufactured tableware and inexpensive novelties used as give-away premiums. During the 1950s, the company took advantage of the national interest in early American reproductions and milk glass to reproduce several popular patterns including Moon and Star, Daisy and Button, and Hobnail.

In 1975, the company was purchased by Owens-Illinois and operated as a wholly owned subsidiary. L.E. Smith returned to local ownership in 1986, when it was purchased by Harry Clew, a former Mellon Bank vice president, and George Franconeri, previously with R.C.R. Crystal. Local entrepreneur Michael Carlow bought the company in 1996, then declared bankruptcy. Jay H. Lustig then purchased the firm. It is currently a subsidiary of NBI, Inc. L.E. Smith continues to produce gift and tableware in a broad range of colors.

STOURBRIDGE FLINT GLASS WORKS

1823–1830   John Robinson, Sr.
1830–1836   J.&T. Robinson (or T.&J. Robinson)
1836–1845   Robinson, Anderson & Co.
John Robinson built his glass factory on the corner of Ross and Second streets in 1823. The area, then known as Kensington, is at the eastern end of downtown Pittsburgh. Two years later, Robinson expanded his business adding by another building at Ross and First streets for cutting, etching, and engraving. Two tumblers in the Historical Society of Western Pennsylvania's collection, blown by James Lee, document the quality of the cut and engraved work done at this factory. The 1826 Pittsburgh city directory notes that the firm manufactured only flint glass. In 1827, Robinson obtained a patent for pressing glass knobs for furniture, and shortly thereafter was joined by his sons John and Thomas Robinson; the firm's name was changed to J.&T. Robinson. After John Sr.'s death in 1836, his sons took in Alex Anderson and the name was changed again to Robinson, Anderson & Co., before the company disbanded in 1845.

American Bottles and Flasks and Their Ancestry attributes several flasks to the Stourbridge factory. The two portrait flasks are of George Washington and Andrew Jackson and date 1824 to 1828. The scroll flasks date slightly later, 1830-34, and are embossed with "JR. & S" or "JR & SON." Stourbridge is also known for its salt dishes in the shape of steamboats. These are inscribed on the stern "J. Robinson & Son/Pittsburgh" or simply "Pittsburgh." A small, pressed plate with scalloped edges and a wreath of oak leaves also bears the inscription "T&J Robinson/Pittsburgh."

TIBBY BROTHERS

1866–1870s?   Factory at 22nd and Smallman streets, Pittsburgh
1873–1914   Factory on Main Street, Sharpsburg

Four Tibby brothers — James, John, William, and Matthew — were partners in the original Pittsburgh works. According to a family history, James left the company shortly after the company's formation and returned to making nails, his previous trade. Contemporary billheads note that the Tibby Brothers manufactured flint glass vials and bottles. The Historical Society's archival collections include a number of invoices for vials sent to Dr. James McClelland, a prominent Pittsburgh physician.

American Bottles and Flasks and Their Ancestry states that Ireland was the birthplace of all the Tibbys except William, who was born in Pennsylvania. The Pittsburgh firm must have been successful from the start. All of the brothers had substantial personal or real estate holdings. In 1871, Matthew Tibby moved to Sharpsburg, a few miles north of Pittsburgh on the north shore of the Allegheny River. There he supervised construction of a second factory between Main Street and the river at about 22nd Street, just a few blocks from the H. J. Heinz family home. It is uncertain how long the Pittsburgh factory remained in operation. The 1882 atlas shows the factory owned by William McCully.

A description of the firm in *Allegheny County, Pennsylvania; Illustrated* (1896) notes the Tibby Brothers trade was nationwide. The factory's capacity increased several times in its first decade of operation. Beginning at the Sharpsburg plant with one 10-pot furnace, they added a second furnace in 1875 and a third one in 1881. The company's production included prescription vials, pickle and milk jars, catsup and beer bottles, and flasks. By the late 19th century, in addition to the original three brothers, the firm included four of their sons: James Renwick Wilson Tibby, who later became president of the firm; James Sloan Tibby; John Knox Milligan Tibby; and William Cooper Tibby.

In 1905, the Pennsylvania Railroad began to buy property along the Allegheny River in Sharpsburg with the intention of relocating its tracks from the old canal bed further north in the borough. According to the family history noted above, by Martha Gillespie Tibby, the railroad purchased the factory property in 1914, closing out the company's history.

UNITED STATES GLASS CO. (U.S. Glass)

1891–1963   U.S. Glass Co.

Fifteen glass companies which were primarily tableware producers merged to form United States Glass Co. Initially the conglomerate included Adams and Co., Pittsburgh; Bryce Brothers, Pittsburgh; Challinor Taylor, Tarentum; George Duncan and Sons, Pittsburgh; Richards & Hartley, Tarentum; Ripley and Co., Pittsburgh; Gillinder & Sons, Greensburg; Hobbs Glass Co., Pittsburgh; Columbia Glass Co., Findlay, Ohio; King Glass Company, Pittsburgh; O'Hara Glass Co., Pittsburgh; Bellaire Goblet Co., Findlay, Ohio; Nickel Plate Glass Co., Fostoria, Ohio; Central Glass Co., Wheeling, W. Va.; and Doyle & Co., Pittsburgh. A.

J. Beatty & Sons of Tiffin and Steubenville, Ohio, then joined the conglomerate in 1892.

In 1893, U.S. Glass purchased about 500 acres along the east shore of the Monongahela River near McKeesport to build a two-furnace, fireproof glass plant. The factory and surrounding community were developed by the company as Glassport. The Glassport facility produced bar goods, stemware, and high-grade tableware.

U.S. Glass also produced specialty items. During the 1896 and 1900 presidential campaigns, the company produced commemorative tumblers, goblets, busts, and plates which featured the candidates' portraits. State stemware patterns were first made in 1897 (Illinois, Kentucky, Maryland, Minnesota, Pennsylvania); again in 1898 (Colorado, Indiana, Massachusetts, Minnesota); and in 1900 (Connecticut, Iowa, New Jersey, Texas).

The pressed ware operation for tumblers, beer mugs, jellies, and tableware was relocated from the Tiffin plant to a new plant in Gas City, Ind., in 1897. In 1909, U.S. Glass established another pressed and blown glass factory for making tableware and specialties in Connellsville, Pa. The Tiffin plant by the mid-1920s became the company's flagship plant for blown ware: lead glass tumblers, stemware, and fancy cut glass. Occasionally U.S. Glass pieces are found bearing the mark "USGC."

During the Depression, many of the factories in the conglomerate closed. By 1931, only five plants operated in the Pittsburgh area (Factories A, B, D, K on Pittsburgh's South Side, and Glassport). In 1937, the corporate offices moved from Pittsburgh to Tiffin, Ohio. The company continued to liquidate selected operations during the 1940s. Due to bankruptcy, the Tiffin plant ceased in 1962 to operate as part of U.S. Glass. Finally, a tornado destroyed the Glassport plant in 1963.

WESTMORELAND GLASS CO.

1889–1925   Westmoreland Specialty Glass Co.
1925–1984   Westmoreland Glass Co.

Westmoreland Specialty Glass was incorporated October 14, 1889, when two brothers, George and Charles West, joined George Irwin to purchase a recently completed factory from a firm known as Specialty Glass Co. in Grapeville, Westmoreland County. The factory was next to the Pennsylvania

Railroad line in farmland about 25 miles east of Pittsburgh. In 1891, Irwin left the enterprise, and Ira Brainard, a Pittsburgh neighbor and an acquaintance of the Wests', joined the firm. In the early years, the company manufactured containers for food such as mustard, pickles, and candy.

In 1921, ownership of the company shifted when George West resigned. Ira Brainard took over as president and brought on his son James Brainard to serve as treasurer. George West stayed in the trade, forming a glass decorating firm in nearby Jeannette. The 1925 name change to Westmoreland Glass Co. more clearly expressed the company's general consumer glass line. Charles West left the firm in 1936 and the Brainard family ran the company from then until it closed in 1984.

In his *Westmoreland Glass* (1996), Charles West Wilson, grandson of Charles West, reports the company made a stunning variety of tableware and decorative items of every description — bowls, plates, compotes, candlesticks, pitchers, and vases — during nearly 100 years of operation. Early on, Westmoreland made glass in many colors and was noted for its decorations. The company produced blanks which were then cut or engraved. Other pieces were enameled with sprays of flowers. As Wilson notes, new molds were expensive but new decorations were not. Applied decoration was one way Westmoreland distinguished itself from competitors.

After the Brainard family took over in the late 1930s, they instituted a number of changes to make the company more profitable. They focused on the best-selling lines, deleting less popular items, and restricted colored glass to "antique blue" — an opaque or milk glass. Westmoreland also began to focus on reproduction pieces, reusing old molds. In the 1940s and '50s milk glass (opaque white glass) became very popular and Westmoreland reached its peak sales years, producing it in every shape and form. Wilson states that in 1957, roughly 95 percent of Westmoreland's sales was milk glass. In the 1960s, as the milk glass craze faded, the company began to produce colors again.

President J. H. Brainard sold the company in the early 1980s to David Grossman, and the plant shut down in 1984. Equipment and materials were auctioned and the building was sold again, this time as a storage facility. The building burned in a February 1996 fire.

YOUGHIOGHENY OPALESCENT GLASS CO.

| 1976 | Youghiogheny Opalescent Glass Co., Connellsville, Pa. |
| 1995 | Added Youghiogheny Art Glass line |

Prior to founding Youghiogheny Glass, John Triggs managed the glass color division of General Color and Chemical in Minerva, Ohio. The company made concentrated colors to supply a range of manufacturers of glass, ceramics, and plastics. When he left General Color to start his own company in 1976, Triggs had "a handful of money and big dreams." He would use his expertise in concentrated color to create opalescent glass for makers of stained glass products, artists, and hobbyists.

Triggs struggled in the first few years. In 1977, fire devastated the young (and under-insured) business. It was not until 1978 that he was able to resume normal production, grossing less than $100,000 that year. From two full-time employees in 1978, Youghiogheny Glass has expanded to employ (in 1998) a staff of 16 full-time workers, with an annual gross income of more than $2 million. About 50 percent of his sales are to Asia (to manufacturers in China and for the hobby business in Japan, in particular) and to Europe, with the remainder in U.S. sales across the country.

In 1995, Triggs joined forces with Steve Fenstermacher to create a second division, Youghiogheny Art Glass. Fenstermacher grew up in Corning, N.Y., and became the youngest apprentice ever to be taken on at Steuben Glass and the youngest ever to have his own chair as gaffer. He spent 17 years at Steuben before following John Potts to Lenox in Mt. Pleasant, where Potts became plant manager. When Potts left Lenox less than two years later, Fenstermacher began looking for a new studio situation, landing at Youghiogheny. Over his career, he has created the wedding chalice for the marriage of the Duke and Duchess of York, inaugural bowls for presidents Reagan, Bush, and Clinton, and complex designs for prestigious corporate awards for companies such as Minute Maid, for the Western Pennsylvania Society of Engineers, and others.

Glass Factories in the Pittsburgh Region

1837

All Along the Rivers

By 1837, there were 28 glass factories in Western Pennsylvania. Fifteen factories were located within the city of Pittsburgh and another 13 were situated to the south and east in Washington and Fayette counties. All were linked by river to raw material sources and to markets near and far. Even at this early date, a wide range of items was produced, including window glass, bottles, lamps, scientific glassware, and tableware.

PITTSBURGH
NORTH SIDE
ALLEGHENY RIVER
LIBERTY AVE.
GRANT ST.
DOWNTOWN
MONONGAHELA RIVER
SOUTH SIDE

ALLEGHENY RIVER

OHIO RIVER

ALLEGHENY

Pittsburgh

PENNSYLVANIA

WASHINGTON

• Elizabeth
Monongahela City • • Williamsport
• Belle Vernon
• Fayette City
Redstone • • Perryopolis
• Brownsville
• Bridgeport

MONONGAHELA RIVER

GREENE

FAYETTE

• New Geneva

OHIO

WEST VIRGINIA

MI NY VT NH MA
OH PA CT RI
NJ
MD DE
KY WV VA
TN NC

Glass Factories in the Tri-State Region

1902

Factories All Around

By 1902, there were over 100 glass factories in the region. Most factories were located far beyond the city: throughout Western Pennsylvania, in the panhandle of West Virginia, and in eastern Ohio. Factory owners preferred open spaces for building larger plants. Natural gas, available since the 1880s in outlying areas, provided an affordable, clean-burning fuel for the industry. Wherever gas surged below ground, factories rose above. The spreading tentacles of the railroad also freed glass factories from their dependence on the river system.

OHIO

ALLEGHENY RIVER

WARREN

Bradford   Eldred   Shinglehouse
Smethport   Port Allegany   Walton
Mt. Jewett   McKEAN   Coudersport
Sheffield   Hazelhurst   POTTER
Kane
Wilcox

ELK

CLARION

Brookville   Falls Creek
Reynoldsville   Du Bois
JEFFERSON
New Bethlehem

PITTSBURGH AREA
SHARPSBURG
ALLEGHENY RIVER
NORTH SIDE   STRIP DISTRICT
OAKLAND   SWISSVALE
OHIO RIVER   DOWNTOWN
MONONGAHELA RIVER
SOUTH SIDE   HOMESTEAD

New Castle
LAWRENCE   BUTLER
Ellwood City   Butler
Zelienople
Beaver Falls
N. Rochester   Rochester   Hites
BEAVER   Monaca   Tarentum
Creighton   Arnold
Glenshaw   Springdale
Coraopolis   Oakmont
Steubenville   ALLEGHENY
Wellsburg   Bridgeville   Pittsburgh
McDonald
Bridgeport   Washington   Glassport
Martins Ferry   OHIO   New Eagle
Wheeling   Monongahela City   Belle Vernon
Bellaire   WASHINGTON   Charleroi

Kittanning   INDIANA
Ford City
ARMSTRONG
Indiana
Saltsburg
Blairsville   CAMBRIA   Altoona
WESTMORELAND   BLAIR
Jeannette   Latrobe
Grapeville
Mt. Pleasant
Everson
Brownsville
Uniontown   SOMERSET   BEDFORD

PENNSYLVANIA

Everett

GUERNSEY

Barnesville
Byesville   Quaker City
NOBLE

Moundsville
Cameron
MONROE   GREENE

New Martinsville   MONONGAHELA R.
WETZEL
Sistersville
Mannington
TYLER   Fairmont
MARION
HARRISON   TAYLOR
Salem   Clarksburg
DODDRIDGE   BARBOUR

WEST VIRGINIA

Point Marion
Morgantown

Buckhannon
UPSHUR

MI NY VT NH MA
OH PA CT RI
NJ
WV MD DE
KY VA
TN NC

Index